Better Writing

Mary T. Carbone

THOMSON

SOUTH-WESTERN

Australia · Canada · Mexico · Singapore · Spain · United Kingdom · United States

THOMSON

™

SOUTH-WESTERN

Better Writing
Mary T. Carbone

VP/Editorial Director:
Jack W. Calhoun

VP/Editor-in-Chief:
Karen Schmohe

Acquisitions Editor:
Jane Phelan

Project Manager:
Penny Shank

Consulting Editors:
Carol Ruhl
Elaine Langlois

Marketing Manager:
Valerie Lauer

Production Editor:
Cami Cacciatore

Manufacturing Coordinator:
Kevin Kluck

Production House:
Cadmus Professional Communications

Printer:
Banta Book Group
Harrisonburg, Virginia

Art Director:
Stacy Jenkins Shirley

Internal Designer:
Beckmeyer Design, Inc.

Cover Designer:
Beckmeyer Design, Inc.

Cover Photo:
©Getty Images

For more information about our products,
contact us at:

Thomson Higher Education
5191 Natorp Boulevard
Mason, Ohio 45040
USA

Asia (including India)
Thomson Learning
5 Shenton Way
#01-01 UIC Building
Singapore 068808

Australia/New Zealand
Thomson Learning Australia
102 Dodds Street
Southbank, Victoria 3006
Australia

Canada
Thomson Nelson
1120 Birchmount Road
Toronto, Ontario
M1K 5G4
Canada

Latin America
Thomson Learning
Seneca, 53
Colonia Polanco
11560 Mexico
D.F. Mexico

UK/Europe/Middle East/Africa
Thomson Learning
High Holborn House
50/51 Bedford Row
London WC1R 4LR
United Kingdom

Spain (including Portugal)
Thomson Paraninfo
Calle Magallanes, 25
28015 Madrid, Spain

Part ① The Sentence

Contents

Part ② Grammar

Part ④ Spelling

Part ⑤ Style

$\bigcirc$REFACE

Better Writing presents a new method of teaching and learning about the sentence, grammar, punctuation, spelling, and style. It is based on two facts: (1) before students can learn to write well, they need to learn to write correctly, and (2) learning to write correctly—and effectively—can be made easy.

The presentation of this new method is timely. Across the nation, students are graduating—even from college—without the necessary writing skills. Surveys reveal that students do not know basic grammar rules or how to construct a proper sentence. *Better Writing* is an answer to these concerns. By means of the Five-Way Method, it presents not only *what* to know but also *how* to write in an organized way for easier and more effective writing.

The Five Ways

Part 1   **The Sentence.** Knowledge of the sentence provides the necessary background for understanding grammar, punctuation, and the advanced work of style.

Part 2   **Grammar.** The grammar section eliminates technical language and unnecessary theory, emphasizing the most common errors to ensure that writers never make these mistakes.

Part 3   **Punctuation.** Learning critical rules on how to punctuate the simple, compound, and complex sentence and doing special exercises to form correct habits can help eliminate errors.

Part 4   **Spelling.** *Better Writing* provides easy-to-remember clues for spelling problem words, helping students learn to spell them correctly.

Part 5   **Style.** This section gets writers to think about the words they use and the ways in which they construct their sentences, paragraphs, and compositions. It presents the great principles of unity, coherence, and emphasis in teaching students how to write well.

Objectives

Better Writing is intended for an introductory English or composition course. It can be used for both classroom instruction and independent study. After completing the text, students will be able to

- Understand and apply basic rules of grammar and punctuation.
- Write unified, coherent, and emphatic sentences, paragraphs, and compositions.
- Think and write critically, keeping an open mind on questions until all the facts are in.

Better Writing can also serve as a complete reference guide to grammar, punctuation, style, and writing. Even after they have completed the textbook, students should be encouraged to continue to use it at home, at school or college, or at their place of employment.

Special Features

Better Writing presents not only *what* to know in our language but also *how* to use it for easier, more effective writing. The following features of the text help improve writing skills:

- **The Sentence in Three Stages** is a special step-by-step program that gives students a proper knowledge of the sentence. Stage 1: Recognize the subject and verb in a sentence. Stage 2: Recognize the subject, verb, and "completer" of a sentence. Stage 3: Recognize phrases and clauses as subjects; identify the main subject and verb in a sentence with a modifying clause.

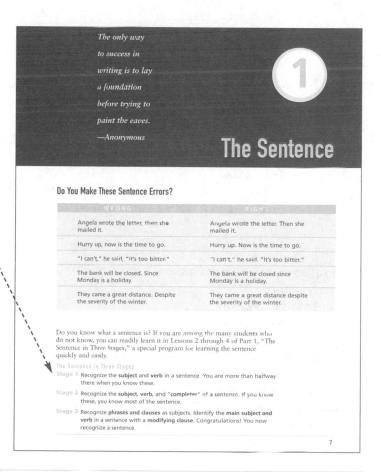

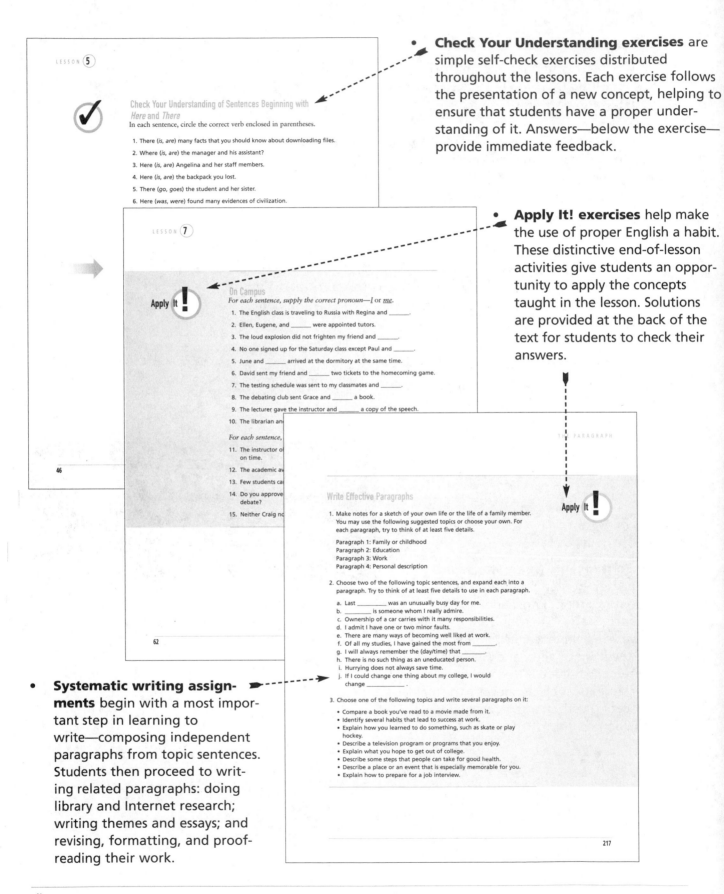

LESSON 5

Check Your Understanding of Sentences Beginning with
Here and *There*
In each sentence, circle the correct verb enclosed in parentheses.

1. There (*is, are*) many facts that you should know about downloading files.
2. Where (*is, are*) the manager and his assistant?
3. Here (*is, are*) Angelina and her staff members.
4. Here (*is, are*) the backpack you lost.
5. There (*go, goes*) the student and her sister.
6. Here (*was, were*) found many evidences of civilization.

LESSON 7

Apply It!

On Campus
For each sentence, supply the correct pronoun—I or me.

1. The English class is traveling to Russia with Regina and _____.
2. Ellen, Eugene, and _____ were appointed tutors.
3. The loud explosion did not frighten my friend and _____.
4. No one signed up for the Saturday class except Paul and _____.
5. June and _____ arrived at the dormitory at the same time.
6. David sent my friend and _____ two tickets to the homecoming game.
7. The testing schedule was sent to my classmates and _____.
8. The debating club sent Grace and _____ a book.
9. The lecturer gave the instructor and _____ a copy of the speech.
10. The librarian and

For each sentence,

11. The instructor o
    on time.
12. The academic a
13. Few students ca
14. Do you approve
    debate?
15. Neither Craig no

46

62

THE PARAGRAPH

Write Effective Paragraphs

1. Make notes for a sketch of your own life or the life of a family member. You may use the following suggested topics or choose your own. For each paragraph, try to think of at least five details.

   Paragraph 1: Family or childhood
   Paragraph 2: Education
   Paragraph 3: Work
   Paragraph 4: Personal description

2. Choose two of the following topic sentences, and expand each into a paragraph. Try to think of at least five details to use in each paragraph.

   a. Last _____ was an unusually busy day for me.
   b. _____ is someone whom I really admire.
   c. Ownership of a car carries with it many responsibilities.
   d. I admit I have one or two minor faults.
   e. There are many ways of becoming well liked at work.
   f. Of all my studies, I have gained the most from _____.
   g. I will always remember the (day/time) that _____.
   h. There is no such thing as an uneducated person.
   i. Hurrying does not always save time.
   j. If I could change one thing about my college, I would
      change _____ .

3. Choose one of the following topics and write several paragraphs on it:

   • Compare a book you've read to a movie made from it.
   • Identify several habits that lead to success at work.
   • Explain how you learned to do something, such as skate or play
     hockey.
   • Describe a television program or programs that you enjoy.
   • Explain what you hope to get out of college.
   • Describe some steps that people can take for good health.
   • Describe a place or an event that is especially memorable for you.
   • Explain how to prepare for a job interview.

Apply It!

217

• **Check Your Understanding exercises** are simple self-check exercises distributed throughout the lessons. Each exercise follows the presentation of a new concept, helping to ensure that students have a proper understanding of it. Answers—below the exercise—provide immediate feedback.

• **Apply It! exercises** help make the use of proper English a habit. These distinctive end-of-lesson activities give students an opportunity to apply the concepts taught in the lesson. Solutions are provided at the back of the text for students to check their answers.

• **Systematic writing assignments** begin with a most important step in learning to write—composing independent paragraphs from topic sentences. Students then proceed to writing related paragraphs: doing library and Internet research; writing themes and essays; and revising, formatting, and proofreading their work.

IMPROVE YOUR VOCABULARY
Prefixes and Roots

AD: to, at, toward

Ad means *to* or *at* as *ad*join, to join to, and *toward* as advise, to look toward. This prefix may become *a, ac, af, ag, al, an, ap, ar, as,* or *at* as in *a*scent, *ac*cede, *af*fix, *ag*grandize, *al*lot, *an*nex, *ap*peal, *ar*rest, *as*sume, and *at*tract.

Adjacent, *to*; adjoining. (*jacere,* to lie)
Admire, to wonder *at*; to esteem highly. (*mirari,* to wonder)
Admonish, to warn *toward*; reprove mildly. (*monere,* to warn)
Affable, to speak *to*; pleasant, friendly. (*fari,* to speak)
Affluent, to flow *to*; an abundance. (*fluere,* to flow)

Examples

The house *adjacent* to yours lies next *to* it.

To *admire* a person means literally to wonder *at* him.

When parents *admonish* a child, they warn him *toward* avoiding some fault or wrongdoing.

Being pleasant and friendly in conversation, *affable* people are easy to speak *to.*

A person to whom money seems to flow *to* with little effort may be considered *affluent* or wealthy.

Other words for recognizing prefixes and roots: adage, aggression, allege, alleviate, alliteration, appraise, arrogant.

Vocabulary Check

Match words with definitions by placing the correct letter in each blank.

____	1. adjacent	a.	to warn; caution
____	2. admire	b.	near; close to
____	3. admonish	c.	easy to be spoken to; courteous; kind
____	4. affable	d.	rich
____	5. affluent	e.	to regard with strong approval, delight, or wonder
		f.	allowable

26

Improve Your Vocabulary features are designed to improve students' reading and writing ability. Vocabulary development contributes to improved reading and better writing.

Clearness is the
fundamental
quality of style,
a quality so
essential in every
kind of writing
that for want of it,
nothing can atone.
—Hugh Blair,
1783

5
Style

Do You Make These Mistakes in Writing?

WRONG	RIGHT
Use fancy words to impress others.	Use simple, specific words.
Write wordy sentences.	Condense elements, and delete unnecessary words.
Present the same thought twice.	Eliminate sentences with the same thought unless for emphasis.
Write childish sentences.	Vary the length, beginnings, forms, and kinds of sentences.
Write skimpy paragraphs.	Supply sufficient details and particulars to support a topic sentence.
Compose difficult-to-read works.	Use the great principles of Unity, Coherence, and Force to write clearly and forcefully.

Clearness, clearness, clearness. Clearness *is* the prize in writing and is always the mark of a good style. Force, the ability to express ourselves in such a way as to make it likely our readers will remember what we have said, is also important.

Fortunately, you need to know only several principles—the great qualities of Unity, Coherence, and Force, or Emphasis—in order to be able to write in a good style. In the following lessons, you will learn how to apply these principles to improve your writing.

183

Style principles guide students as they move beyond writing correctly to writing well—developing a polished and effective style. The eight lessons in Part 5 focus on the great qualities of writing—unity, coherence, and emphasis—and their use in constructing sentences, paragraphs, and compositions. The section on Practical Suggestions for Writing, or the writing process, provides an overview of essential issues of style and a simple five-step process for producing better writing, from planning to finished work.

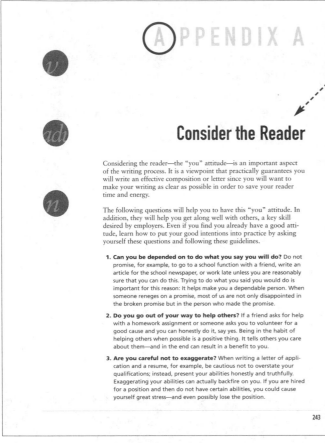

Consider the Reader—or the "you" attitude—is an important aspect of the writing process. The questions and insights in this special appendix will help students cultivate the "you" attitude and apply it in their interactions with others and their writing.

Better Writing is a systematic, self-paced method of learning how to write. This text is an essential resource for students who want to improve their writing skills and boost their career potential.

Acknowledgments

The author is grateful to the following individuals who reviewed the manuscript and offered suggestions:

Michael F. Courteau, The Art Institutes International Minnesota, Minnesota, MN

Elaine Giuliano, Central Coast College, Salinas, CA

Jennifer E. Marano, Silicon Valley College, Fremont, CA

Donna McCullough, Wood Tobe-Coburn School, New York, NY

Sara L. Morgan, Minnesota School of Business, Plymouth, MN

Emma L. Tan, ASA Institute of Advanced Technology, Brooklyn, NY

Carolyn Varvel, Art Institute of Colorado, Denver, CO

> *We must study not*
> *only that every hearer*
> *may understand us,*
> *but that it shall be*
> *impossible for him not*
> *to understand us.*
> *—Quintilian, circa*
> *A.D. 35–95*

Practical Suggestions for Writing

Do You Make These Mistakes in Writing?

WRONG	RIGHT
Begin writing without careful thought.	Plan your writing. Decide on your purpose, and continue to think about why you are writing until you have finished.
Attempt to write without getting all the facts.	First get the facts.
Send off your work without checking it.	Set your work aside, and later reread it.
Be neglectful of your reader's interests.	Consider your reader, above all making sure your writing is clear.
Focus more on fancy writing than on the thought of your message.	Realize that the thought of your message is the more important part of your writing.

Have you had much writing experience? Do you feel confident in your ability to express yourself? In this introductory section, you will find practical suggestions for writing—especially helpful if you have not had much practice in writing. You will learn rules for not only thinking and writing in an orderly and efficient way but also for having good interpersonal skills and for thinking critically—invaluable skills especially needed for the workplace.

The more detailed problems of writing—the sentence, grammar, punctuation, spelling, and style—are addressed in Parts 1, 2, 3, 4, and 5. You first, however, need a natural background for their discussion, which you will find here in Practical Suggestions for Writing.

Practical Suggestions for Writing

These practical suggestions for writing are often referred to as the **writing process.**

1. Plan Your Writing

Begin by thinking about what you will be writing. If it is an assignment, look closely at the directions, and note any key words.

Decide on your purpose. Think carefully about what you want to say, and, if possible, choose a subject you know about or in which you are interested. For a composition, it could be to explain something or give advice on a subject. For a letter, it will usually be to persuade someone to do something. Keep thinking about why you are writing until you have finished. For unless your purpose is clear in your mind, it will be no better in the reader's mind.

Get all the facts. Facts are the core of composition. You cannot take too many pains in gathering facts. You would never deceive yourself with the idea that you can dash off a composition in a short time without knowing anything about the subject. An old verse, though, might help remind you that the greatest achievement awaits the person knowing the most facts:

> *F is for Facts; you will scribble in vain*
> *If a grip on these churls you don't get and retain.*

Outline. For a simple theme or letter, it does not have to be elaborate; a listing of key points is usually fine. Some compositions, however, require a great deal of thought to make them understandable.

2. Note the Three Aspects of Good Writing

While not always included in the writing process, these three aspects are a significant part of it.

Be yourself. Study the works of the best authors, a necessity for not only gaining an understanding of how to write in a good style but for supplying yourself with a stock of words on different subjects. But have confidence in your ability to express yourself. You do not need an unusual sensitivity to people nor a great facility with words or the ability to write similes and metaphors. What you do need is to be yourself and write sincerely and truthfully.

Consider the reader. Called the "you" attitude, a caring viewpoint practically guarantees that you will write an effective composition or letter. Above all, you will want to make your writing as clear as possible in order to save your reader time and energy. Add the day of an appointment—*Wednesday*, June 28—for example, to reduce the possibility of error.

Before you can hope to write successful messages, you will want to make sure you have a good attitude towards others. You will find these guidelines in Appendix A. Fairness and tact, though, deserve special mention here.

Be fair. We cannot be fair if we are concerned only with ourselves. It has been said, in fact, that unfairness is usually the result of selfishness. Although fairness is considered especially important in letters intended to adjust differences, there are many opportunities to be honest and fair.

Be tactful. Tact, the special ability to relate to others in such a way so as not to hurt their feelings, summarizes all the other qualities and deserves special mention. If someone present, for example, is overweight, the tactful person will refrain from any reference to weight loss programs. The Golden Rule—do unto others, as you would have them do unto you—is perhaps the best definition of this important quality.

Think critically. Pay more attention to the thought of your message than to its style. What you say—the thought of your message—is the more important part of your writing. It is essential, therefore, to be in the habit of thinking critically and judging fairly on every problem.

What is critical thinking? Mainly, it involves thinking about all sides of an issue, continually questioning assumptions, and not being afraid to change your mind despite what others may think. It can apply to every subject—education, business, ethics, politics, science, and the like. Thinking critically can be best defined as keeping an open mind on every question until all the facts are in.

Critical thinking in the workplace. A study conducted by Jean-François Manzoni and Jean-Louis Barsoux and discussed in *The Set-Up-To-Fail-Syndrome: How Good Managers Cause Great People to Fail* (Harvard Business School Press, 2002) shows the importance of critical thinking in business problems. According to the authors of the study, managers are often at fault when an employee fails. The authors found that what can happen is that the employee might receive a less-than-enthusiastic recommendation from a former employer, the manager then will distrust the employee, and the employee will respond by losing confidence and performing less well.

According to the authors of the study, managers could have ended the cycle by keeping an open mind and asking these critical questions: Is the employee's performance as bad as I think it is? Could there be other factors, aside from performance, that have caused me to label this person a weak performer? Did we hire this person because of above-average qualities? And, if so, why have those qualities disappeared?

What is required for critical thinking, then, is the ability to think through an issue instead of being content to simply form an opinion. How can you equip yourself to make sound judgments? How can you become a critical thinker instead of a merely well-informed person? You can begin by asking yourself the following three questions, or questions like them, every day. These questions are often called the ABCs of Education:

A. Do I really want to know the truth about something, or do I want to prove only that the ideas I already have are correct?

B. Am I willing to consider the possibility that I could be wrong in my judgment of an issue?

C. Have I ever thought about the reasons for my most treasured opinions? That is, can I plainly seek the truth about something despite where it might lead me?

Remember, it is the thought of your message—what you say—that is the more important part of your writing. No matter what you write about, therefore, you need to have a technique such as the ABCs of Education to be able to find the truth—and become truly educated. You need some way to be able to see the "other side of the story."

The final step. The final step, then, is to weigh each sentence, paragraph, and message and question yourself about the truth of each. Are my facts correct? Is it possible I could be wrong about this? Even if you ask only these questions, you will be well on your way to making sound judgments.

3. Compose

Do not worry too much about minor details at this stage. At the same time, compose slowly and with care, especially in following the great principles of writing: Unity, Clearness, Force, and Emphasis.

Unity. A sentence should present only one thought; a paragraph, one topic; and a composition, one subject. Supplying sufficient facts and eliminating unnecessary ones is the key to unity of the paragraph and composition.

Clearness. Above all, a sentence should be clear. The term "coherence" (a sticking together) is often used in place of clearness to refer to the paragraph and composition.

Force. Force is the quality that makes sentences sound mature and sophisticated, not childish and choppy. Elements such as the use of conciseness, active verbs, and putting something before the subject help you gain this vital quality. The use of clear, forceful words also contributes to this key quality.

Emphasis. Emphasis is the powerful aid to force, a quality that can be attained by placing important parts at the beginnings and endings of sentences, paragraphs, and whole messages.

4. Revise

The secret of success in writing effectively lies in the careful improvement of your work. After writing, set your work aside, and later reread it as if it belonged to someone else. If possible, have someone else read your work and suggest how it could be improved. Now is the time for abolishing redundancies, for arranging your sentences correctly, for checking for incorrect grammar and punctuation, and for bringing style into a consistent and effective form.

5. Prepare Your Finished Copy

Make your writing look professional. Whether you are writing a business letter or a theme, correctness in form suggests accuracy and efficiency and influences your reader's estimate of you and your ability. Proofread carefully to make sure your document is error free, and check the appearance of each page. In addition, place your name, date, and other information properly on your theme to make it easy for your instructor to identify your work—and gain a good impression of you.

Summary

1. **Plan your writing.**

   Decide on your purpose. Remember, unless your purpose is clear in your mind, it will be no better in your reader's.

   Get all the facts. Facts are the core of composition.

   Outline. For a simple theme or letter, a listing of key points is usually fine.

2. **Note the three aspects of good writing.**

   Be yourself. Study the works of the best authors, but have confidence in your ability to express yourself and write sincerely and truthfully.

   Consider the reader—the "you" attitude. Above all, make your writing as clear as possible to save your readers their time and energy. Study Appendix A, Consider the Reader. The twelve questions there will help you develop the "you" attitude. In addition, these guidelines will help you get along well with others, a key skill desired by employers.

   Think critically. Keep an open mind on every question until all the facts are in.

3. **Compose.** When composing, keep in mind the great principles of writing—Unity, Clearness, Force, and Emphasis.

4. **Revise.** Always reread your work to improve it and to check for any inconsistencies.

5. **Prepare your finished copy.** First impressions count! Follow the guidelines for making your work look professional—and give a good impression of yourself.

*The only way
to success in
writing is to lay
a foundation
before trying to
paint the eaves.*

—Anonymous

The Sentence

Do You Make These Sentence Errors?

WRONG	RIGHT
Angela wrote the letter, then she mailed it.	Angela wrote the letter. Then she mailed it.
Hurry up, now is the time to go.	Hurry up. Now is the time to go.
"I can't," he said, "it's too bitter."	"I can't," he said. "It's too bitter."
The bank will be closed. Since Monday is a holiday.	The bank will be closed since Monday is a holiday.
They came a great distance. Despite the severity of the winter.	They came a great distance despite the severity of the winter.

Do you know what a sentence is? If you are among the many students who do not know, you can readily learn it in Lessons 2 through 4 of Part 1, "The Sentence in Three Stages," a special program for learning the sentence quickly and easily.

The Sentence in Three Stages

Stage 1 Recognize the **subject** and **verb** in a sentence. You are more than halfway there when you know these.

Stage 2 Recognize the **subject**, **verb**, and "**completer**" of a sentence. If you know these, you know most of the sentence.

Stage 3 Recognize **phrases and clauses** as subjects. Identify the **main subject and verb** in a sentence with a **modifying clause**. Congratulations! You now recognize a sentence.

7

PART 1 PRETEST

In the space provided, write one of the following letters (A, B, or C) to identify the correct answer in each sentence.

(A) sentence (B) two sentences written as one (C) part of a sentence

1. I have never supported tax increases. _____

2. As you did. _____

3. The purpose of a sales letter, however, is motivation. _____

4. Ann sent her resume to the company, then she called the human resources director. _____

5. That is not true. _____

6. As you already know, the downtime will be less with private companies. _____

7. The mark grew larger finally we saw the sign. _____

8. The speaker received much applause. _____

9. Since his speech was a masterpiece. _____

10. It is a mistake of course it is. _____

11. You should remember that otherwise you would seem rude. _____

12. Please remember that specialists gave you these tests. _____

13. And that there are many ways of answering the questions. _____

14. We were pleased when you became a member, however, we noticed that your membership recently lapsed. _____

15. To open the file, you must have a special password. _____

16. Being a chief executive officer who managed a well-furnished office. _____

17. Looking forward to hearing from you. _____

18. I really should hurry to the office. _____

19. Otherwise, I might be late. _____

20. They passed the examination, therefore they were happy. _____

The Parts of Speech

1a	**Noun**	A <u>noun</u> is the name of something.
1b	**Pronoun**	A <u>pronoun</u> takes the place of a noun.
1c	**Verb**	A <u>verb</u> shows action or indicates a state or condition.
1d	**Adjective**	An <u>adjective</u> modifies a noun or pronoun.
1e	**Adverb**	An <u>adverb</u> modifies a verb, an adjective, or another adverb.
1f	**Conjunction**	A <u>conjunction</u> is a joining word.
1g	**Preposition**	A <u>preposition</u> shows a relation as "<u>with</u> respect" or "<u>in</u> our nation."
1h	**Interjection**	An <u>interjection</u> expresses strong feeling.

Contrary to what some might say, you really do need to be familiar with the parts of speech—if only to have the terminology for understanding how to improve and revise sentences. A shortcut to knowing the parts of speech is to learn by heart the names of *linking verbs*, *helping verbs*, *conjunctions*, and *prepositions*.

1a Noun

A **noun** is the name of a person, place, or thing. The word "thing" is used not only for objects that we can see, hear, taste, or touch but also for words such as *patriotism*, *sorrow*, and *peace*. In the following passage, the italicized words are the names of various objects called nouns.

> The *art* of separating a *person* from his *money* is a delicate *matter*, and all the *tact* and *diplomacy* of which a skillful *salesperson* is *master* will not ward off every *complaint*. *Discontent* arises from *carelessness* in giving or in filling an *order*.

1b Pronoun

A **pronoun** takes the place of a noun. The following are commonly used *personal pronouns*:

> I, me, he, him, she, her, we, us, they, them, it, you, who, whom

You should be familiar with other pronouns in common use, a list of which follows. Whenever you are uncertain whether a word is a pronoun, refer to this list. In a short time, you will be familiar with most of them.

Other Pronouns

each	those	some	everyone
every	all	same	someone
either	any	both	somebody
neither	one	several	something
this	other	few	much
that	another	anybody	many
these	none	everybody	which

1c Verb

A **verb,** the most important word in the sentence, shows action or indicates a state or condition.

For *action verbs*, however, the action does not necessarily imply motion, such as *run, jump,* and *skip*. Action verbs can also be actions of the mind, such as *think, consider,* and *remember*.

> The consultant *wrote* many letters.
> The members *concentrated* their efforts on winning the argument.

Those that do not express action (*linking verbs*) make a statement and also connect or link the subject with the word or words that follow it. The primary linking verbs follow:

is	am	are	was	were	been
feel	look	appear	become	seem	remain

Andres *was* a student.   Jane *became* a friend.
I *remain* an avid reader.   The cold ice *felt* good.

A verb may not always be a single word but sometimes a group of words, such as "Your order *has been sent*." The following twenty-three words are *helping verbs*. (The first eight are also linking verbs.)

Helping Verbs

is	be	may	does
am	being	can	did
are	shall	have	could
was	will	has	would
were	must	had	should
been	might	do	

1d Adjective

An **adjective** modifies or in some way makes the meaning of a noun or pronoun more exact. An adjective can describe a noun (the *rocky* ledge) or limit a noun (*two* dollars).

They worked in a *busy* office.
He bought the *latest* version of the software.
Mr. Ito designed the *company* database.

1e Adverb

An **adverb** modifies a verb, an adjective, or another adverb. Adverbs usually answer the questions *how*, *when*, *where*, *why*, or *to what extent* and often end in -ly.

They read books *often*. (Describes a verb)
They were *very* close friends. (Describes an adjective)
They worked *really* well together. (Describes an adverb)

Although an adverb often modifies the verb in the sentence, it is not always placed directly after the verb. At times, it is placed between the parts of the verb phrase.

> They <u>were</u> *desperately* <u>looking</u> for a dictionary.
> The child <u>was</u> *happily* <u>walking</u> in the rain.
> The company <u>could</u> *easily* <u>hire</u> six new employees.

1f Conjunction

Conjunctions are connecting words that join sentences, clauses, phrases, or words.

Coordinating conjunctions connect elements of equal rank. They are

and, or, nor, but, yet, for, so

> The staff meets on Monday, *and* the workers meet on Friday.
> Courage is admirable, *but* patience is powerful.
> Ty knows word processing, *yet* he wants to take a refresher course.

Be sure to memorize the seven coordinating conjunctions. When you can recall them, you will automatically know when to place a comma in a compound sentence.

Subordinating conjunctions connect elements of unequal rank. They introduce dependent clauses and are important because they can remind you to place a comma after the clause.

> *If* a letter is too long, it wastes the time of the correspondent and the reader.
> *After* my money was gone, I no longer had friends.

The following mnemonic (a means used as an aid in remembering) will help you recall these key words:

Aunt	*Betty*	*is*	*smarter*	*than*	*Uncle*	*Wally.*
after	because	if	since	than	unless	when
although	before			though	until	where
as						while

1g Preposition

A **preposition** shows a relation to some other word in the sentence.

> The president *of* the company reported an increase in sales.

The word *of* not only connects the two nouns president and company but shows the relation between them; the president belongs to the company. If you omit *of*, you no longer know what the president and the company have to do with each other.

Prepositions

about	at	but	in	past	up
above	before	by	into	since	upon
across	behind	concerning	like	thought	with
after	below	down	near	to	
against	beneath	during	of	toward	
along	beside	except	off	under	
among	between	for	on	underneath	
around	beyond	from	over	until	

Ten prepositions used more frequently than the others are

> in, on, for, from, at, to, by, of, like, with

1h Interjection

An **interjection** expresses strong feeling.

> Oh! My computer just crashed!
> Hey! Do you know where you're going?
> Wow! That was a great movie!

Note: The part of speech to which a word belongs is determined by its use in the sentence.

> May I *open* the window? (Verb)
> We came at last to *open* country. (Adjective)
> I always enjoy hiking in the *open*. (Noun)

Apply It !

The Parts of Speech

For each sentence, circle the italicized word that identifies the speech part.

Facts are the foundation of permanent knowledge.

1. Facts	*noun*	*adjective*	*adverb*
2. are	*noun*	*adjective*	*verb*
3. foundation	*noun*	*adjective*	*adverb*
4. of	*noun*	*preposition*	*adjective*
5. permanent	*verb*	*preposition*	*adjective*
6. knowledge	*noun*	*adjective*	*verb*

A certainty points one way.

7. certainty	*noun*	*adjective*	*pronoun*
8. points	*verb*	*adverb*	*noun*
9. one	*verb*	*adjective*	*adverb*
10. way	*verb*	*adjective*	*noun*

Necessity is a good teacher.

11. Necessity	*verb*	*adjective*	*noun*
12. is	*noun*	*adverb*	*verb*
13. good	*noun*	*adjective*	*adverb*
14. teacher	*noun*	*adjective*	*verb*

IMPROVE YOUR VOCABULARY
Prefixes and Roots

A **prefix** is a letter, syllable, or word added to the beginning of some other word to vary or modify its meaning, while a **root** is the main part of the word. In the word *absolve*, for example, *abs* is the prefix meaning from, and *solv* is the root, or main part, meaning loosen.

A, AB, ABS: from, away

A, *ab*, or *abs* means *from*: *a*vert, to turn *away* from; *ab*solve, to release from; *abs*tract, to draw from.

> *Ab*dicate, to proclaim *from*; give up. (*dic*, *dict*, to proclaim)
> *Ab*hor, to shudder *from*; shrink back *from* in dread or horror.
>   (*horrero*, to shudder)
> *Ab*solve, to loosen *from*; to free from guilt. (*solv*, to loosen)
> *Abs*cond, to conceal *from*; leave secretly. (*condo*, to conceal)
> *Abs*truse, thrust *away*; hard to understand. (*trudere*, to thrust)

Examples

The manager *abdicated* his responsibilities, withdrawing *from* his various duties.

To *abhor* is to hate with loathing, literally a shrinking back *from*.

Absolve means to set free or release *from* some duty or obligation.

Abscond does not mean to take someone's money but to run *away* secretly.

Students found some *abstruse* points in philosophy, statements hidden *away* from their understanding.

Other words for recognizing prefixes and roots: aberrant, abnegate, absent, abstemious.

Vocabulary Check

Match words with definitions by placing the correct letter in each blank.

_____ 1. abdicate   a. to hate, loathe
_____ 2. abhor   b. to flee in haste and in secret
_____ 3. absolve   c. to await, endure
_____ 4. abscond   d. obscure; hidden away from understanding
_____ 5. abstruse   e. to withdraw from duties; to give up formally
                    f. to set free or release; to forgive

Lesson ②

Subject and Verb (Stage One)

This lesson covers the most important parts of the sentence, subjects and verbs.

2a	Verbs of one word.	*They <u>returned</u> to the computer lab.*
2b	Verbs of more than one word.	*They <u>had gone</u> to Hawaii the previous year.*
2c	Verbs, not modifiers.	*The student <u>was</u> not present.*
2d	Finding the subject.	*The <u>caravan</u> started on its journey.*
2e	Compound subjects and verbs.	*<u>Michael</u> and <u>George</u> <u>ran</u> and <u>swam</u>.*
2f	Compound sentences.	*<u>I</u> <u>lost</u> my ring, and my <u>friend</u> <u>found</u> it.*

A sentence is a group of words expressing a complete thought. It has a **subject** and **predicate** (the words that make a statement about the subject), with the core word of the subject usually being a **noun** or **pronoun** and the core word of the predicate being a **verb.** Most importantly, be sure you are able to find the verb of the sentence easily.

2a Verbs of One Word

A verb may be one word. It may be either an *action verb* or a *linking verb*.

> The students *greeted* each other. (Action verb)
> A blank space *means* a missing design. (Action verb)
> The thesis *provides* an overview of the major points. (Action verb)
> Planners usually *remember* every element of the plan. (Action verb)

Many action verbs, such as *provides* and *remember*, do not seem to be moving or doing anything, but they are action verbs.

You'll recall from Lesson 1 that linking verbs connect or link the subject with the word or words that follow it. The linking verbs are *is*, *am*, *are*, *was*, *were*, *been*.

> The graphics software *is* new. (Linking verb)
> I *am* happy with my keyboarding class. (Linking verb)
> The windows *are* open. (Linking verb)
> They *were* friends. (Linking verb)

Check Your Understanding of Verbs of One Word

Underline the verb in each sentence.

1. The other check-out lines at the grocery store always move faster.

2. Unfortunately, the warranties on our office printers expire after one year.

3. Nature always sides with the hidden flaw.

4. A shortcut is the shortest distance between two points.

5. The formatting of business letters differs from that of other kinds of correspondence.

6. The beginning and ending of the body of the letter is the most difficult part of the message.

7. The date of a letter consists of the month, day of the month, and year.

8. Never use red ink for writing letters.

9. An elegant letter is less common than any other specimen of composition.

10. The renovation embraces the whole concept of an open office design.

Answers: 1. move 2. expire 3. sides 4. is 5. differs 6. is 7. consists 8. use 9. is 10. embraces

2b Verbs of More Than One Word

A verb may not always be a single word but sometimes a group of words, such as "Your order *has been sent.*" Review the list of helping verbs. Then study the sentences.

Helping Verbs

is	been	must	has	could
am	be	might	had	would
are	being	may	do	should
was	shall	can	does	
were	will	have	did	

The students *greeted* each other. (One word)
Jane *has written* a thesis. (Two words)
They *had been living* in Chicago. (Three words)

Check Your Understanding of Verbs of More Than One Word

Underline the verb in each sentence, and circle the number of words in each.

1. The consultant wrote many letters.	1	2
2. The students finished the test.	1	2
3. Leo was an assistant.	1	2
4. Each step is easy.	1	2
5. The office assistant struck the keys with the proper fingers.	1	2
6. A writer should use specific words.	1	2
7. Writers should have a high regard for accuracy.	1	2
8. They are shipping the goods today.	1	2
9. Recipes should include shortening.	1	2
10. The letter had been sent early.	2	3
11. The door had been hinged at the top.	2	3
12. The checks should be written plainly.	2	3
13. They had been working an hour.	2	3
14. The work should have been done sooner.	3	4

2c Verbs, Not Modifiers

Words that tell something about the verb are not part of the verb. They may be very important to the meaning of the sentence. Nevertheless, they are not part of the verb. Study the following sentences:

> The story <u>was</u> *not* true. (Can you *not*?)
> The patio <u>was laid</u> *out* in blocks. (Can you *out*?)
> Students *carefully* <u>study</u> for exams. (Can you *carefully*?)

Not, *out*, and *carefully* tell something about the verb and are not part of it. Only *was*, *was laid*, and *study* are verbs in the preceding sentences.

Words that tell something about the subject are also not part of the verb. Certain linking verbs are frequently followed by **modifiers** that describe the subject. In the first sentence, for example, *cold* describes the subject *night*.

> The night <u>was</u> *cold*. (Can you *cold*?)
> The guards <u>had become</u> *careless*. (Can you *careless*?)
> He <u>was</u> *hungry*. (Can you *hungry*?)

Again, *cold*, *careless*, and *hungry* are not part of the verb. Only *was*, *had become*, and *was* are verbs.

Check Your Understanding of Verbs, Not Modifiers

Underline the verb—and nothing but the verb—in each sentence.

1. The loan application must be filled out completely.

2. The self-help book is full of good suggestions.

3. The student had never read the procedures for using the Internet.

4. A half-truth is often a great lie.

5. The layers must be firmly glued together.

6. The software documentation is usually divided into sections or parts.

7. The plane was rapidly gaining altitude.

8. The action plan should be implemented immediately.

9. They were fairly safe.

10. An ergonomic workstation has been set up for each new employee.

Answers: 1. must be filled **2.** is **3.** had read **4.** is **5.** must be glued **6.** is divided **7.** was gaining **8.** should be implemented **9.** were **10.** has been set

2d Finding the Subject

Always find the verb first. Then ask *who* or *what* about the verb. The answer is the subject.

A noun or pronoun usually serves as the simple subject, the simple subject being the particular word in the complete subject about which something is said.

Phrases That May Interfere

A frequent error is to consider the object of the prepositional phrase the subject of the sentence.

>   The *managers* in our office <u>are</u> capable professionals.

In the preceding sentence, *managers* is the subject, and *are* is the verb. *In our office*, a prepositional phrase, tells something about managers. *Office*, the object of the preposition *in*, is NOT the subject of the sentence.

A prepositional phrase may include smaller phrases:

>   The chimney sits <u>on the top</u> <u>of the house</u>.
>   1   2

Two phrases may also modify separately:

>   Turn <u>to the right</u> <u>at the next corner</u>.
>   1   2

Remember, no part of a prepositional phrase can be a subject. To avoid taking the wrong word for the subject, eliminate all prepositional phrases by crossing them out, at least in your mind.

Check Your Understanding of Phrases That May Interfere

Is the underlined word the subject of each sentence? Circle Yes or No. If No, underline the subject.

1. In the past, <u>reports</u> from the office were sent weekly.   yes   no

2. An <u>advantage</u> of the direct plan is its conciseness.   yes   no

3. Your pronunciation of those <u>words</u> is incorrect.   yes   no

4. The <u>management</u> gave all the employees a holiday.   yes   no

5. The <u>secretary</u> of the club read the minutes.   yes   no

6. Paper for <u>letters</u> should be suitable for the purpose.   yes   no

7. My friend in <u>Boston</u> has bought a new computer. yes no

8. The <u>president</u> of the company reported better sales. yes no

9. The style of the <u>letter</u> should be determined beforehand. yes no

10. A <u>variety</u> of copiers was found in the office. yes no

11. The manager in the <u>office</u> introduced the new employees. yes no

12. Many different colors of copier <u>paper</u> are available. yes no

Answers: 1. yes **2.** yes **3.** no/pronunciation **4.** yes **5.** yes **6.** no/paper **7.** no/friend **8.** yes **9.** no/style **10.** yes **11.** no/manager **12.** no/colors

Pronouns as Subjects

You are familiar with pronouns in common use, such as *each*, *every*, *either*, *neither*, and *this*. You might want to refer back to Lesson 1 (1b), though, to review the list of these pronouns. Meanwhile, study the following sentences to see how these pronouns function as subjects.

> *Neither* of the coats fits him. (Subject)
> *Each* of the contestants was right. (Subject)
> *Either* of the job applicants would be successful. (Subject)
> *Anybody* who takes keyboarding acquires a critical skill. (Subject)
> *None* of our computers are infected with the virus. (Subject)
> *This* is the result we all expected. (Subject)

Check Your Understanding of Pronouns as Subjects

In each sentence, underline each subject once and each verb twice.

1. Many of the members of the committee called for a meeting.

2. In the past year, several of the units have been tested.

3. Only one of the contestants finished the race.

4. Most of the inhabitants were prepared for the invasion.

5. Everyone in the room knows the reason for the test.

6. Unfortunately, someone in the class has already seen the movie.

7. Neither of the students has a right to the tickets.

8. Last summer both of the contestants applied for the scholarship.

Answers: 1. Many/called **2.** several/have been tested **3.** one/finished **4.** Most/were prepared **5.** Everyone/knows **6.** someone/has seen **7.** Neither/has **8.** both/applied

Varied Order of the Subject

The subject may not always be before the verb. It may, in fact, be anywhere in the sentence. Study the following sentences:

> Down <u>jumped</u> the *cat*. (The *cat* <u>jumped</u> down.)
> <u>Are</u> *you* sure? (*You* <u>are</u> sure.)

The subjects of most interrogative (questioning) sentences are not in their natural order. To find the subject, it may be necessary to change the interrogative sentence to declarative form.

> <u>Who</u> is that person? (That person is <u>who</u>.)
> <u>What</u> do you want? (You want <u>what</u>.)

In sentences introduced by *there* or *it*, the subject follows the verb. *Here* and *there* are used as fillers. They merely introduce.

> There <u>is</u> *Donald Harney*. (*Donald Harney* <u>is</u> there.)
> Here <u>are</u> the computer *disks*. (The computer *disks* <u>are</u> here.)

The subject of a command sentence is usually omitted. *You* (the subject) is understood.

> [You] Lock the office door by six o'clock.
> Do not [you] forget.

Check Your Understanding of Varied Order of the Subject

In each sentence, underline each subject once and each verb twice.

1. Forget about the Outstanding Athlete Award.

2. There will be several applicants for the position of Web Page Designer.

3. How are you voting this time?

4. Here is the account of one of the witnesses.

5. How cold the wind is tonight!

6. From these strikes came new labor laws.

7. Turn to the right at the first intersection.

Answers. 1. [You] Forget 2. applicants/will be 3. you/are voting 4. account/is 5. wind/is 6. laws/came 7. [You] turn

2e Compound Subjects and Verbs

A sentence may have a compound subject, a compound verb, or both. "Compound" simply means to be made up of two or more parts.

Study the following sentences:

> The *doctor* and her *aides* are planning to go.
> The manager *keyed* the letter and *mailed* it.
> *Spring* and *summer came* and *went*.

In the first sentence the subject—*doctor* and *aides*—is compound. In the second sentence the verb—*keyed* and *mailed*—is compound. And in the third sentence, both subject and verb are compound.

Check Your Understanding of Compound Subjects and Verbs

Write S (for subject) if the underlined compound unit is the subject and V (for verb) if the unit is the verb in each sentence.

1. Its <u>success</u> and <u>popularity</u> encouraged other investors.

2. The speaker <u>presented</u> the awards and <u>discussed</u> plans for future awards.

3. <u>Instructors</u> and <u>employees</u> recognize the importance of good keyboarding skills.

4. <u>Janet</u> and <u>Martha</u> are friends.

5. <u>Carlos</u> and his <u>neighbors</u> sell notebook computers.

6. Mark <u>owns</u> and <u>runs</u> a computer center.

7. She <u>went</u> to the window and <u>looked</u> out at the gathering storm clouds.

8. Carissa <u>buys</u> and <u>sells</u> stock.

9. The passers-by <u>stopped</u> and <u>stared</u> at the little monkey.

10. The <u>coach</u> or his <u>assistants</u> are planning to go to the tournament tomorrow.

11. Lewis <u>found</u> the package and <u>removed</u> the wrapping.

12. *Upload* and *download* are familiar computer terms.

Answers: 1. success, popularity–subject **2.** presented, discussed–verb **3.** Instructors, employees–subject **4.** Janet, Martha–subject **5.** Carlos, neighbors–subject **6.** owns, runs–verb **7.** went, looked–verb **8.** buys, sells–verb **9.** stopped, stared–verb **10.** coach, assistants–subject **11.** found, removed–verb **12.** *Upload, download*–subject

2f Compound Sentences

A *compound sentence* makes two complete statements. These are joined by a comma and a coordinating conjunction or by a semicolon.

Use a comma to separate the two statements of a compound sentence only when the second statement begins with a coordinating conjunction (and, or, nor, but, yet, for, so).

> I am going to the conference, *and* you can join me.
> Friends come and go, *but* enemies accumulate.
> Shelly will attend the workshop, *or* she will send a substitute.
> He has a fine reputation, *yet* I do not know him personally.
> Nedla did not pass the exam, *nor* will she graduate.

Use a semicolon in a compound sentence when the second statement begins with any word other than a coordinating conjunction.

> *I* <u>saw</u> Harvey yesterday; *he* <u>was</u> very happy.
> The *president* <u>introduced</u> the speaker; then *she* <u>sat</u> down.
> *Lori* <u>is</u> working on her degree; *Emma* <u>has</u> hers.
> *Sales* <u>are</u> good; *we* <u>expect</u> a profit.

Check Your Understanding of Compound Sentences

Underline each subject once and each verb twice in each sentence.

1. Beth is not tired, yet she has worked hard.

2. I saw him yesterday, and he seemed happy.

3. Selma may consider your recommendation, or she may disregard it.

4. This backpack is good for carrying books; everyone should try it.

5. I am going to the meeting, but you can come along.

6. It does not matter; I am not tired now.

7. I did not seek the position, nor do I want it.

8. We had no assignments, so we left.

9. They had nearly finished the task, but they did not go on break.

10. Jim is well liked, for he has many good qualities.

Answers: 1. Beth/is, she/has worked **2.** I/saw, he/seemed **3.** Selma/may consider, she/may disregard **4.** backpack/is; everyone/should try **5.** I/am going, you/can come **6.** It/does matter; I/am **7.** I/did seek, I/do want **8.** We/had, we/left **9.** They/had finished, they/did go **10.** Jim/is liked, he/has

Stage One of the Sentence

In each sentence, underline the subject once and the verb twice.

Apply It!

1. The day was warm.

2. Opportunities for improvement are offered by the Human Resources Department.

3. Neither of the videos has been ordered.

4. The company has not purchased a new site for its new regional office.

5. They smiled cordially and continued on their way.

6. The container of gas soon cooled and solidified.

7. Many of the tickets to the hockey game were sold.

8. Did the president report an increase?

9. The amount of money was substantial.

10. Letters and gifts pour into the studio.

11. Sound the alarm!

12. There is a new manager.

13. Your ticket for the swimming competition is not stamped; therefore, it is invalid.

14. They practiced every morning, but they had little success.

15. Their charges for going online are minimal; however, a tax is required.

IMPROVE YOUR VOCABULARY
Prefixes and Roots

Ad means *to* or *at* as *ad*join, to join to, and *toward* as advise, to look toward. This prefix may become *a, ac, af, ag, al, an, ap, ar, as,* or *at* as in *a*scent, *ac*cede, *af*fix, *ag*grandize, *al*lot, *an*nex, *ap*peal, *ar*rest, *as*sume, and *at*tract.

> *Ad*jacent, *to*; adjoining. (*jacere*, to lie)
> *Ad*mire, to wonder *at*; to esteem highly. (*mirari*, to wonder)
> *Ad*monish, to warn *toward*; reprove mildly. (*monere*, to warn)
> *Af*fable, to speak *to*; pleasant, friendly. (*fari*, to speak)
> *Af*fluent, to flow *to*; an abundance. (*fluere*, to flow)

Examples

The house *adjacent* to yours lies next *to* it.

To *admire* a person means literally to wonder *at* him.

When parents *admonish* a child, they warn him *toward* avoiding some fault or wrongdoing.

Being pleasant and friendly in conversation, *affable* people are easy to speak *to*.

A person to whom money seems to flow *to* with little effort may be considered *affluent* or wealthy.

Other words for recognizing prefixes and roots: adage, aggression, allege, alleviate, alliteration, appraise, arrogant.

Vocabulary Check

Match words with definitions by placing the correct letter in each blank.

_____ 1. adjacent   a. to warn; caution
_____ 2. admire   b. near; close to
_____ 3. admonish   c. easy to be spoken to; courteous; kind
_____ 4. affable   d. rich
_____ 5. affluent   e. to regard with strong approval, delight, or wonder
            f. allowable

Subject, Verb, and "Completer" (Stage Two)

This lesson covers the second stage of learning the sentence.

3a	**Subject complements after linking verbs.**	*John's diction was <u>flawless</u>.*
3b	**Direct objects after action verbs.**	*The bee stung <u>Jackie</u>.*
3c	**Subjects and verbs, not adjectives and adverbs.**	*The friendly <u>student</u> quietly <u>left</u>.*
3d	**Verbs, not verbals.**	*<u>People</u> digging for clams <u>should expect</u> wet feet.*

The three parts of the sentence are **subject, verb,** and **completer,** a **completer** being a word that completes the meaning of the verb. "Completers" of linking verbs are *subject complements*, and "completers" of action verbs are *direct objects*.

3a Subject Complements After Linking Verbs

A linking verb always requires a noun, a pronoun, or an adjective (a subject complement) to complete its meaning.

> Easy credit <u>is</u> a *temptation* to extravagance. (Noun)
> The winner of the contest <u>was</u> *she*. (Pronoun)
> The strawberries <u>are</u> *fresh*. (Adjective)

In the first sentence, the simple subject is the noun *credit*, and the verb is *is*. The noun *temptation* is the subject complement of the verb *is* and completes its sense.

In the second sentence, the simple subject is the noun *winner*, and the verb is *was*. The pronoun *she* is the subject complement of the verb *was* and completes its sense.

In the third sentence, the simple subject is the noun *strawberries*, and the verb is *are*. The adjective *fresh* is the subject complement of the verb *are* and completes its sense.

Check Your Understanding of Subject Complements After Linking Verbs

Underline the linking verb, and circle the subject complement in each sentence.

1. Kelly is a teacher.

2. Everything was quiet in the offices.

3. The street has become muddy.

4. That is an economical car.

5. The account was theirs.

6. In general, reports are impersonal.

7. Albuquerque is the capital of New Mexico.

8. Australia is a continent.

9. The audience seems restless.

10. Old-fashioned typewriters are cumbersome.

3b Direct Objects After Action Verbs

Some action verbs do not require nouns or pronouns to complete their meaning.

Birds *fly*.   The rain *fell*.
The employees *complained*.   Grasshoppers *jump*.

Most action verbs, however, require a noun or pronoun—*a direct object*—to complete their meaning. Direct objects either receive the action or show the result of the action.

They usually <u>bring</u> the *reports* with them. (Noun)
The engineer <u>questioned</u> *them*. (Pronoun)

In the first sentence, the simple subject is the pronoun *They*, and the verb is *bring*. *Reports* is the direct object of the action verb *bring* and completes its sense.

In the second sentence, the simple subject is the noun *engineer*, and the verb is *questioned*. *Them* is the direct object of the action verb *questioned* and completes its sense.

Check Your Understanding of Direct Objects After Action Verbs

Underline each verb, and circle its direct object in each sentence.

1. The student refused the invitation.

2. The company purchased several printers.

3. We bought these books at the fair.

4. The judge examined the files.

5. Studying takes time.

6. Marvin has learned his lesson.

7. The architect built a building.

8. The dean writes many letters.

9. We received your telegram.

Answers. 1. refused/invitation 2. purchased/printers 3. bought/books 4. examined/files 5. takes/time 6. has learned/lesson 7. built/building 8. writes/letters 9. received/telegram

3c Subjects and Verbs, Not Adjectives and Adverbs

If you can recognize adjectives and adverbs, you can more easily find the subject and verb by seeing what is *not* the subject or verb.

Adjectives The following sentences show the adjectives in italics.

> A *little* learning is a *dangerous* thing.
> The gift was *valuable*.

Although adjectives usually occur directly before the nouns they describe, they can follow linking verbs as in the sentence *The gift was* <u>*valuable*</u>.

Check Your Understanding of Adjectives

Cross out all adjectives. Underline the subject once and the verb twice in each sentence.

1. The tiresome journey was now at an end.

2. Kyle spoke to an enthusiastic audience.

3. Jasmine did not remember her first attempts to swim.

4. A large crowd gathered at the student center.

5. The next day the convention took a formal vote.

Answers: 1. (tiresome) journey/was 2. (enthusiastic) Kyle/spoke 3. (first) Jasmine/did remember 4. (large) crowd/gathered 5. (next, formal) convention/took

Adverbs Adverbs are not difficult. You will find it helpful, though, to remember that, unlike adjectives, they can be moved around in a sentence. Notice the position of the adverbs in the following sentences:

> The study of the classics is *definitely* needed.
> They added a room to their business *recently*.
> *Sometimes* I use the computer in the office downstairs.

Check Your Understanding of Adverbs

Cross out all adverbs. Underline the subject once and the verb twice.

1. Diane always does her work well.

2. They were looking desperately for an unabridged dictionary.

3. The checks should be written plainly.

4. The weather is extremely cold.

5. They work well together.

6. The problem was solved correctly.

3d Verbs, Not Verbals

Every sentence needs a verb, and a verbal cannot fill in for this crucial part of speech. A verbal cannot act as a verb, the only similarity between verbs and verbals being that **verbals** can take direct objects or subject complements or any of the modifiers that a verb might have.

There are three kinds of verbals: those that end in *–ing* and *–ed* and those introduced by *to*.

declin*ing* values   *revised* edition   *to* keyboard

In the following sentences, verbs are underlined, while verbals are italicized.

I <u>enjoyed</u> *visiting* him.
Georgia <u>was seated</u> in a room *containing* a table and chair.
Sue <u>likes</u> *to read* novels.

Again, you should be able to see that such words as *visiting* or *containing* or *to read* are not true verbs.

Check Your Understanding of Verbals

Is the underlined word the verb? If not, underline the verb in each sentence.

1. The dog, <u>barking</u>, frightened the child.   yes   no

2. Asher <u>ran</u> to see the parade.   yes   no

3. The person <u>walking</u> down the aisle is my friend.   yes   no

4. She did not see the <u>deleted</u> word.   yes   no

5. The moving train suddenly <u>came</u> to a halt.   yes   no

6. This <u>is</u> a factor to be noted.   yes   no

7. Grumbling, the old man sat down.   yes   no

8. The computer virus spread quickly.   yes   no

9. Smiling broadly, the student read the evaluation.   yes   no

10. Bradley appreciated sitting in the front row.   yes   no

Answers: 1. no/frightened 2. yes 3. no/is 4. no/did see 5. yes 6. yes 7. no/sat 8. yes 9. no/read 10. no/appreciated

Stage Two of the Sentence

In each sentence, underline the subject once and the verb twice; circle any subject complement or direct object the sentence may have.

1. The managers in our office are capable professionals.

2. Students at the college can easily learn their lessons.

3. Your pronunciation of those words is incorrect.

4. The workers in the office received a good bonus.

5. I do not understand the performance appraisal.

6. The bookkeeper found several errors in the account.

7. The manager carefully drew the plan.

8. Recently, we added a large room to our house.

9. She presented a valuable gift to the winner.

10. The crackling fire warmed their hands.

11. The limping scout followed the parade.

12. The leaves, fluttering, dropped to the ground.

13. They walked to the cottage in their dripping clothes.

14. He manages a thriving business.

15. The football game was exciting.

IMPROVE YOUR VOCABULARY
Prefixes and Roots

ANTE: before

Ante means *before* as *ante*cedent, going before, and *ante*diluvian, before the flood.

> *Antebellum, before* the war. (*ante bellum*, before the war)
> *Antecedent*, going *before*; prior; previous. (*cedere*, to go)
> *Ante* meridian, *before* midday. (*meridies*, noon)
> *Anteroom*, the room *before* the main room.
> *Anticipate*, to deal with *beforehand*.

Examples

Antebellum usually refers to the time *before* the Civil War.

The *antecedent* of a pronoun should match the noun or pronoun to which it refers or goes *before*.

The abbreviation *a.m.* stands for *ante meridian*, *before* midday.

Many offices have *anterooms*, through which clients pass *before* entering the main room.

"Do not *anticipate* trouble" means "Do not expect trouble *before* it comes."

Other words for recognizing prefixes and roots: ancestors, antediluvian, antenatal.

Vocabulary Check

Match words with definitions by placing the correct letter in each blank.

_____	1. antebellum	a.	that which goes before
_____	2. antecedent	b.	a room that precedes another
_____	3. ante meridian	c.	before noon
_____	4. anteroom	d.	to look forward to; to expect
_____	5. anticipate	e.	a remedy for poison
		f.	before the war

Subjects, Verbs, Phrases, and Clauses (Stage Three)

4a	**Verbal phrases as subjects.**	*Playing sports* took all their time.
4b	**Clauses as subjects.**	*What they want* is difficult to know.
4c	**The subject and verb in a sentence with a modifying clause.**	As we reached the top of the hill, *we saw* the river.
4d	**Explanatory words (appositives).**	Bill Michaels, *an employee of the company*, was at the meeting.

In Stages One and Two of the sentence, you learned about the subject, verb, and "completer." In Stage Three, you will learn to recognize **phrases** and **clauses** so that they will not interfere with your finding the main verb of a sentence. You will soon have achieved your goal of learning the sentence—more quickly and easily than you could have imagined.

4a Verbal Phrases as Subjects

A *verbal phrase* is made up of a verbal and the words used to complete its meanings or modify it. Most often, we think that only a noun or pronoun can be a subject. As you will see in the following sentence, however, the subject is the phrase *Learning new software*, and the verb is *is*.

> *Learning new software* <u>is</u> often required. (Subject)

A verbal phrase can also be a subject complement or a direct object. The following italicized phrases are the subjects of each sentence, with the verbs underlined.

> The job of the sales manager <u>is</u> *promoting sales*. (Subject complement)
> Juanita <u>would like</u> *to study marketing*. (Direct object)

A verbal phrase can also be used as a modifier:

> *Having lost his ticket,* Jack <u>returned</u> home. (Modifier)

In the preceding sentence, the verb is underlined. The italicized phrase has a "verbal" but not a true verb. Try asking yourself if "having lost his ticket" makes complete sense. It does not, and therefore *having lost* could not be the verb.

Check Your Understanding of Verbal Phrases as Subjects

Underline the subject once and the verb twice in each sentence.

1. Keeping warm took all their efforts.

2. Using a computer can be time consuming.

3. To tell the truth is the only alternative.

4. Being a counselor requires considerable tact.

5. Saying nothing is often better than speaking.

6. To promote sales is the job of the sales manager.

7. Buying a gift is usually a pleasant task.

8. Watching a lacrosse game is their favorite pastime.

9. Installing software can be a challenge.

4b Clauses as Subjects

The following sentences demonstrate how a clause can be used as a subject. Words that introduce noun clauses are *that, whether, what, how, why, if, when, where, who,* and *which*.

> *What he wants* <u>is</u> difficult to determine. (Subject)
> *That she would approve the plan* <u>was</u> doubtful. (Subject)

In the first sentence, the subject is the clause *What he wants*, and the verb is *is*. In the second sentence, the subject is the clause *That she would approve the plan*, and the verb is *was*. You need to be able to recognize the subject of a sentence whether it is a noun, a noun phrase, or a noun clause.

Like the noun phrase, a noun clause can also be a subject complement and a direct object.

> This is *what I want*. (Subject complement)
> They asked *who I was*. (Direct object)

Check Your Understanding of Clauses as Subjects

Underline the subject once and the verb twice in each sentence:

1. What I want is this one.

2. That it will rain today is likely.

3. How you manage your income is a mystery.

4. That a mistake had occurred was evident.

5. Whether you stay or go is of little importance.

6. What you want is not here.

7. That they would buy the computers is doubtful.

8. What the chairperson proposed was not practical.

Answers. 1. What I want/is **2.** That it will rain today/is **3.** How you manage your income/is **4.** That a mistake had occurred/was **5.** Whether you stay or go/is **6.** What you want/is **7.** That they would buy the computers/is **8.** What the chairperson proposed/was

4c The Subject and Verb in a Sentence with a Modifying Clause

A *modifying clause* is a dependent clause—a group of words with a subject and predicate that does not make complete sense. The subject and verb of a modifying clause therefore cannot be the real subject

and verb of the sentence. The real subject of the following sentence is *company*, and its verb is *succeeded*.

The company succeeded *because the president was diligent.*

Because the president was diligent is a dependent clause. It does not make sense by itself, depending on *The company succeeded*, a complete sentence, for its logic.

The adjective clause is introduced by such words as *who*, *which*, and *that*.

The apprentice *who is* knowledgeable <u>studied</u> diligently.
The screen saver *that <u>was</u>* downloaded <u>displayed</u> a beach scene.

The adverbial clause is one that acts as an adverb, although this is sometimes hard to see. Adverbial clauses are introduced by subordinating conjunctions: *after, although, as, because, before, if, since, than, though, unless, until, when, where, while.*

After you <u>have reviewed</u> the document, please <u>call</u> us.

Notice that there are two verbs (and two subjects), one in the "dependent" clause and one in the main clause. Notice also the introductory subordinating conjunction *after.*

Check Your Understanding of the Subject and Verb in a Sentence with a Modifying Clause

Underline the main subject once and the main verb twice in each sentence.

1. Mrs. Kuzmina, who is the superintendent, gave a talk.

2. When two people quarrel, both are unhappy.

3. They will find it if they are given the opportunity.

4. As we reached the hill, we saw the river.

5. Dick studies whenever he has a test.

6. We can go tomorrow if the weather is good.

7. After I returned, I prepared the statements.

8. Although we arrived late, we obtained good seats.

4d Explanatory Words (Appositives)

An **appositive** is a word or group of words placed next to another word explaining the same person or thing. It is never the subject.

> Paula, *the manager*, has good communication skills. (Appositive)
> Anthony, *a sales assistant*, has solid editing skills. (Appositive)
> They met with Ryan Lach, *the new graphic artist*. (Appositive)

The first appositive is a single word, the noun *manager*, and the second is two words, a *sales assistant*, *sales* describing *assistant*.

Sometimes the appositive is so closely connected with the noun that no commas are required. It is not good practice to set off the appositive with commas in sentences such as these:

> The poet *Whittier* wrote *Snowbound*. (Appositive)
> My brother *Andrew* is in London. (Appositive)
> The word *telecommunications* is often misspelled. (Appositive)

Check Your Understanding of Explanatory Words (Appositives)

Cross out the appositive in each sentence. Then underline the subject once and the verb twice in the following sentences.

1. Mr. Case, the assistant director, discussed the profit and loss statement.

2. The gold jewelry, a gift from the owner, was lost.

3. Milton, the English poet, wrote *Paradise Lost*.

4. Lee Michaels, an employee of the company, was at the annual meeting.

5. The president, a well-read person, predicted a cost-of-living increase.

6. Ms. Kent, a cost accountant, worked late every evening.

7. My friend, an engineering student, designed the Web site.

8. We, your oldest friends, will help you.

9. Her sister Marsha is in California.

10. The novel *David Copperfield* is considered a classic.

Answers: 1. Mr. Case/discussed **2.** jewelry/was lost **3.** Milton/wrote **4.** Lee Michaels/was **5.** president/predicted **6.** Ms. Kent/worked **7.** friend/designed **8.** We/will help **9.** sister/is **10.** novel/is considered

Stage Three of the Sentence

In each sentence, underline the main subject once and the main verb twice; circle any "completer"—subject complement or direct object.

Apply It !

1. Having completed their homework, the students left early.

2. If Amy has made a mistake, she will correct it.

3. I will be at the station when you arrive.

4. The person who received the medal was my associate.

5. Riding a bicycle can be strenuous.

6. That she is a famous actress is well known.

7. Ms. Tucker, the president of the company, is its founder.

8. With patience, half of the annoyances of life will disappear.

9. Unless you pay your bills promptly, your account will be cancelled.

10. We listened to the television because we wanted to learn the news.

11. People who are thinkers look for facts.

12. Roger brought the books that you ordered.

13. Since you have always helped me, I will secure the loan for you.

14. When it was convenient, they attended the meetings.

15. After you left, the telegram arrived.

IMPROVE YOUR VOCABULARY
Prefixes and Roots

BI: twice, two

Bi means two or twice, as in biped or bicycle.

Bicuspids, two plus pointed end; teeth with two points. (*cuspis*, pointed end)

Biannual, two plus a year; a biannual event occurs twice a year. (*annual*, year)

Bifocals are glasses made with double lenses of different focuses so that the wearer may have one focus for distant vision and one for reading. (*focal*, focal)

Binoculars, two plus ocular eye; using both eyes. (*ocular*, eye)

Bisect, two plus to cut; to cut in two. (*secare*, to cut)

Examples

Bicuspid teeth have *two* points.

A *biannual* convention meets *twice* a year.

Bifocal glasses have *two* lenses.

Binoculars are for using *two* or both eyes in contrast with the telescope, which is a monocular instrument.

In geometry, *bisect* means to cut or divide into *two* parts.

Other words for recognizing prefixes and roots: bicentennial, bilateral, bilingual, biped, bimonthly.

Vocabulary Check

Match words with definitions by placing the correct letter in each blank.

_____ 1. bicuspid   a. to cut into two parts
_____ 2. biannual   b. twice a year
_____ 3. bifocal   c. having two points
_____ 4. binoculars   d. the two hundredth anniversary
_____ 5. bisect   e. having two focal points, as in bifocal glasses
                       f. an instrument for using both eyes

Mend your speech

a little, lest it may

mar your fortunes.

—Shakespeare

Grammar

Do You Make These Mistakes in Grammar?

WRONG	RIGHT
Between you and *I*, I think you are late.	Between you and *me*, I think you are late.
A set of these tools *are* useful.	A set of these tools *is* useful.
The two worked *good* together.	The two worked *well* together.
Each student reviewed *their* work.	Each student reviewed *his* work.
We have *these* kind of cell phones.	We have *this* kind of cell phones.
If I *was* you, I would not go.	If I *were* you, I would not go.
I don't think *me* having been a manager was of help.	I don't think *my* having been a manager was of help.
The patient was urged to *lay* down.	The patient was urged to *lie* down.

Many of us make these errors, errors among the most distracting ones for educated readers. After studying Part 2, however, you will easily be able to avoid such errors—and gain peace of mind in knowing you can write and speak correctly.

Amazingly, you can learn the eight basic grammar rules with a minimum of effort. You do not have to worry about such elements as moods of verbs or the different kinds of pronouns. *With this new and different kind of study, you see right away what the rule is, check your understanding, and practice until your responses become a habit. It is as easy as that.*

5

PART 2 PRETEST

In the space provided, write one of the following letters (A or B) to signify the correct answer in each sentence.

1. Each of these suitcases (A. *has*, B. *have*) been examined. _____

2. The application of this rule (A. *vary*, B. *varies*). _____

3. The company sent the bill to the manager and (A. *I*, B. *me*). _____

4. My associates and (A. *I*, B. *myself*) went to the meeting. _____

5. That collection of papers (A. *is*, B. *are*) valuable. _____

6. Each of the students turned in (A. *his*, B. *their*) report. _____

7. There (A. *is*, B. *are*) a maple and an ash on the property. _____

8. The jury (A. *has*, B. *have*) met in open session. _____

9. Their skis fit (A. *good*, B. *well*). _____

10. Who is the (A. *faster*, B. *fastest*) runner of the two? _____

11. Do you find (A, *this*, B. *these*) kind of day depressing? _____

12. If I (A. *was*, B. *were*) in his place, I would go. _____

13. Ed wishes he (A. *was*, B. *were*) ready to take the position. _____

14. Dena's books are (A. *lying*, B. *laying*) on the desk. _____

15. How long have they (A. *laid*, B. *lain*) there? _____

16. Neither (A. *has*, B. *have*) ever lost a race. _____

17. I have never known of (A. *you*, B. *your*) breaking a promise. _____

18. I did not like (A. *Melissa*, B. *Melissa's*) playing. _____

19. Peter is the (A. *taller*, B. *tallest*) of the twins. _____

20. For (A. *who*, B. *whom*) is this computer intended? _____

Agreement (Level 1)

5a	The subject separated from its verb by a prepositional phrase.	A wide <u>variety</u> of choices <u>is</u> available.
5b	Compound subjects.	Mark <u>and</u> Laura <u>are</u> going. Mark <u>or</u> Laura <u>is</u> going.
5c	Sentences beginning with *here* and *there*.	There <u>are</u> many <u>opportunities</u>.
5d	Collective nouns.	The family <u>is</u> vacationing together. The family <u>are</u> arguing among themselves.
5e	*Each, either*, and *neither*.	<u>Each</u> of the books <u>has</u> sold close to a million copies.
5f	The pronoun and its antecedent.	The college expects every <u>alumna</u> to send <u>her</u> own response.

In Lesson 5, you need to determine whether the subject means one or more than one and then be able to match the verb to it. The noun *variety*, for example, means one and therefore needs to be matched to a verb that means one—*is*. The same applies to a pronoun and the word to which it refers. *Alumna* means one and therefore needs to be matched to a pronoun that means one—*her*.

5a The Subject Separated from Its Verb by a Prepositional Phrase

The verb must agree with its subject. It does not agree with a prepositional phrase or any intervening words between the subject and verb. In the sentence "A box of books was sent to you yesterday," the subject is the noun *box*. The prepositional phrase *of books* merely modifies the subject. You could omit the phrase and still have a complete thought: "A box was sent to you yesterday."

Study the following examples. In each you will find that the prepositional phrase has been placed in parentheses to show that it is not essential to the main idea.

> A *variety* (of foods) *is* to be tested by the FDA.
> A large *supply* (of disks) *is* on the shelves.
> An *assortment* (of appliances) *is* on display.

Note: Sentences such as "The *student*, along with his parents, *was* at the meeting" also take a singular verb.

Tip for Determining Singular or Plural Nouns and Verbs

Most singular nouns add *s* to indicate more than one thing. Notice that *manager* becomes plural by adding *s*. The opposite occurs with certain plural verbs, which indicate more than one thing by dropping the *s*.

> *Singular:*   The manager *calls* the president every day.
> *Plural:*   The managers *call* the president every day.

Check Your Understanding of the Subject Separated from Its Verb

In each sentence, circle the correct verb enclosed in parentheses.

1. The excuse Gene made for his many absences (*was, were*) poor.

2. A complete selection of sizes and styles (*is, are*) ready for shipment.

3. The length of the days and nights (*depends, depend*) on the position and slant of the earth.

4. A variety of categories, from $25 to $100, (*is, are*) available.

5. Their collection of pictures (*is, are*) worth a fortune.

6. The programs for recycling (*appear, appears*) to be effective.

Answers: 1. was **2.** is **3.** depends **4.** is **5.** is **6.** appear

5b Compound Subjects

When two or more subjects are joined by *and* to form one common subject, the verb is usually plural.

> Heather and Rita *are* friends.
> Mrs. Vega and her two assistants *were* planning to attend.

When two or more singular subjects are joined by *or* or *nor*, the verb should be singular. The sentence means *either the one or the other*. It does not mean *both*.

> Sarah *or* Alice *is* going to the meeting.
> Neither the manager *nor* the director *was* responsible for the deficit.

When the subject is composed of both singular and plural subjects joined by *or* or *nor*, the verb should agree with the nearer subject.

> The captain or his *aides are* planning to go.
> Neither friends nor *money was* waiting for me.
> One or more *spreadsheets were* on the floor.

Check Your Understanding of Compound Subjects

In each sentence, circle the correct verb enclosed in parentheses.

1. Clearness and completeness (*is, are*) important qualities.

2. Eric and Marie (*is, are*) planning to attend the auction.

3. Either the agent or the lawyer (*is, are*) going to the meeting.

4. Either Dr. Carey or his assistant (*is, are*) in the office.

5. Printing costs and editing services (*contribute, contributes*) to the high cost of the book.

Answers: 1. are **2.** are **3.** is **4.** is **5.** contribute

5c Sentences Beginning with *Here* and *There*

A common error involves using *There's* instead of *There are* when the subject means more than one.

> *Incorrect*:   There's (There *is*) many pages in this book.
> *Correct*:   There *are* many pages in this book.

Since the subject of the sentence is *pages*, the verb is plural. The adverb *there* does not dictate the number of the verb.

Check Your Understanding of Sentences Beginning with
Here and *There*

In each sentence, circle the correct verb enclosed in parentheses.

1. There (*is, are*) many facts that you should know about downloading files.

2. Where (*is, are*) the manager and his assistant?

3. Here (*is, are*) Angelina and her staff members.

4. Here (*is, are*) the backpack you lost.

5. There (*go, goes*) the student and her sister.

6. Here (*was, were*) found many evidences of civilization.

7. There (*is, are*) six members on the committee.

8. There (*go, goes*) the general with her staff.

Answers. 1. are 2. are 3. are 4. is 5. go 6. were 7. are 8. goes

5d Collective Nouns

Nouns that name a group of persons or a collection of objects are called *collective nouns*. Collective nouns, such as *committee*, *jury*, and *family*, are usually considered singular because the collection is thought of as a whole.

> The *family is* away. (The family is considered as a unit.)
> The *committee was* addressing the topic. (The committee is considered as a unit.)

When the individuals of the group are thought of or act separately, however, they take a plural verb. It is not possible, for example, for one person to argue, discuss, conclude, or the like.

> The *family are* arguing over the report.
> The *committee are* discussing the problem.

Since *one* cannot argue or discuss, the correct verb is *are*.

Check Your Understanding of Collective Nouns

In each sentence, circle the correct verb enclosed in parentheses.

1. The crowd (*was*, *were*) unmanageable.

2. The jury (*was*, *were*) allowed to leave for lunch.

3. The jury (*was*, *were*) arguing among themselves regarding the evidence.

4. The board of directors (*is*, *are*) in session.

5. The faculty (*is*, *are*) recommending changes to the curriculum.

Answers: 1. was 2. was 3. were 4. is 5. is

5e *Each, Either, and Neither*

Each of the following pronouns means only *one* person:

another	anyone	either	everyone	nobody
anybody	each	every	neither	no one
somebody	one			

Since these pronouns are singular, they take a singular verb.

> *Each* of the winners *is* invited to bring a guest.
> *Either* of the players *has* a right to complain.
> *Neither* of the students *speaks* French.

The following pronouns mean *more than one* person and therefore take a plural verb:

many	both	few	several	others

> *Both* of the candidates *are* eligible.
> *Several were* called to the platform.

Check Your Understanding of *Each, Either, and Neither*

In each sentence, circle the correct verb enclosed in parentheses.

1. Neither of the manager's assistants (*was*, *were*) responsible.

2. Either of the assignments (*is*, *are*) too difficult for first-year college students.

3. One in every ten employees (*was, were*) found lacking certain skills.

4. Neither of the answers (*is, are*) correct.

5f The Pronoun and Its Antecedent

Just as a verb should match its subject, a pronoun should match its **antecedent,** the word that "goes before" the pronoun. In the following sentences, each of the subjects means one person; therefore, only pronouns meaning one person should be used.

> If *anyone* wants a CD player, *he* (not they) can get one here.
> *Someone* left *her* (not their) coat in the auditorium.

The problem is that today the rule of using *he* and *him* regardless of gender might not be acceptable to some people. As a result, some may use "they" to avoid the issue. Others may use *he* or *she*, but its use may become awkward as in the following sentence.

> Before an employee files a grievance, *he* or *she* should inform *himself* or *herself* about the consequences.

One answer may be to use a plural pronoun with a plural subject.

> Before *employees* file grievances, *they* should remind themselves about the consequences.

But it may not always be possible to use the plural. Also, it is generally considered more effective to use the singular. One solution is to rewrite the sentence.

> *Original*:   Every coach should have the respect he deserves.
> *Improved*:   Every coach should receive our respect.

Another solution is to leave out the pronoun.

> *Original*:   The student can rely on programmed materials for
>   help with his or her grammar problems.
> *Improved*:   The student can rely on programmed materials for
>   help with grammar problems.

Check Your Understanding of the Pronoun and Its Antecedent

In each sentence, circle the correct verb enclosed in parentheses.

1. Each of the alumnae described (*her*, *their*) first week of classes.

2. If anyone wishes to participate in the teleconference, (*he*, *they*) should say so.

3. The Chamber of Commerce provided the opportunity to learn about the importance of (*its*, *their*) Outreach Program.

4. Someone left (*his*, *their*) pen on my desk.

5. Both students submitted (*his*, *their*) computer literacy report.

6. Northwest Corporation launched (*its*, *their*) advertising campaign.

Answers: 1. her **2.** he **3.** its **4.** his **5.** their **6.** its

Writing for Information

In each sentence, cross out any word used incorrectly, and write the correct form above it. Look for two errors.

Apply It

In writing for information, you need to be clear in your mind as to exactly

what it is you want to know. After you decide this, arrange your letter to make

it easy for your reader to find the items you are requesting. If a variety of points

are being covered, tabulation is often useful.

Requests for routine information should be as brief as possible—

consistent with courtesy and clarity. In writing for a pamphlet, using a

letterhead and keeping your request to the essentials can be of great help.

The quality of stationery and envelopes are important to show that you are in

business or have financial responsibility.

IMPROVE YOUR VOCABULARY
Prefixes and Roots

Circum means *around* or *about* as in *circum*navigate, to sail around.

*Circum*locution, to speak *around*; a round-about way of saying something. (*locu*, to speak)
*Circum*scribe, to draw a line *around*. (*scribe*, to write)
*Circum*spect, to look *about*; cautious; prudent. (*spect*, to look)
*Circum*stance, something attending or *around* an event. (*stare*, to stand)
*Circum*vent, to come *around*; to go around. (*venire*, to come)

Students' activities are much *circumscribed* or limited if they have no car.

Circumspect people are cautious and look *about* themselves "before they leap."

One's *circumstances* are the conditions that "stand *around*" one's life.

By devious dealings, they were able to *circumvent* or go *around* the regulations.

Other words for recognizing prefixes and roots: circumambulate, circumflex, circumvolution.

Vocabulary Check

Match words with definitions by placing the correct letter in each blank.

_____ 1. circumlocution   a. cautious; watchful
_____ 2. circumscribe   b. a roundabout way of speaking
_____ 3. circumspect   c. to enclose within certain lines
_____ 4. circumstances   d. to split
_____ 5. circumvent   e. a condition that affects what happens
                       f. to go around a rule without breaking it

Agreement (Level

6a	**Nouns plural in form but singular in number.**	*Ethics <u>is</u> an interesting subject.*
6b	**Nouns singular in sense but plural in use.**	*The scissors <u>are</u> here.*
6c	***None, any, some, all,*** **and** ***most* (NASAM).**	*All of the <u>students</u> <u>were present</u>.* *All of the <u>money</u> <u>was</u> stolen.*
6d	***The* number and** ***a*** **number.**	*<u>The</u> number of arrests <u>was</u> unusual.* *<u>A</u> number of responses <u>were</u> received.*
6e	***Who*** **and** ***that*** **clauses.**	*Sarah was one of those educators who <u>communicate</u> effectively.*

Here are other instances in which you need to decide whether to use a singular or plural verb. Since it is mostly a matter of determining whether the subject means one or more than one and then matching the verb to it, Lesson 6 presents information about some nouns and pronouns to show whether they should be used as singular or plural.

6a Nouns Plural in Form but Singular in Number

Some nouns are plural in form but singular in number. Most of these words fall into the following classes:

Names of studies such as *ethics*, *physics*, *economics*, and *mathematics*: "*Physics is* an appealing course."

Names of diseases such as *measles*, *mumps*, and *shingles*: "*Measles is* an unpleasant disease."

The title of a book, a play, an opera, and the like: "*The Merry Wives of Windsor is* a play by Shakespeare."

Nouns that designate an amount of money, a unit of measure, or a period of time: "Ten *miles is* a long distance to walk."

Check Your Understanding of Nouns Plural in Form but Singular in Number

In each sentence, circle the correct verb enclosed in parentheses.

1. Microbiology (*is*, *are*) a useful field of study.

2. The news this week (*is*, *are*) startling.

3. Only two thirds of the report (*was*, *were*) finished by the December deadline.

4. Fifty dollars (*is*, *are*) too much to spend for a computer game.

5. "The Tales of Hoffmann" (*is*, *are*) an opera by Jacques Offenbach.

6. Mononucleosis (*is*, *are*) an infectious disease of the blood.

Answers. 1. is 2. is 3. was 4. is 5. is 6. is

6b Nouns Singular in Sense but Plural in Use

Some words, although true singulars, are always used with plural verbs. Among these are *scissors*, *pants*, *shears*, *tongs*, and *pliers*.

The *shears are* very dull.
These *pants are* too short.
Manicure *scissors are* small and sharp.

Check Your Understanding of Nouns Singular in Sense but Plural in Use

In each sentence, circle the correct verb enclosed in parentheses.

1. The forceps (*is, are*) not very sharp.

2. Pliers (*was, were*) left on the desk.

3. The tongs (*was, were*) difficult to maneuver.

4. The contents of the guidebook (*was, were*) clear.

6c *None, Any, Some, All,* and *Most* (NASAM)

None, any, some, all, and *most* are singular or plural according to use. (NASAM spells their initials for easy remembering.) These pronouns do not usually cause difficulty because you automatically correctly match the verb with the object of the preposition. This is an exception to the subject-verb agreement rule to disregard intervening prepositional phrases.

None of the *students were* present.
None of the *chemical was* touched.

Some of the *visitors are* going by plane.
Some of the *dessert is* left.

All of the *trainees were* invited to the conference.
All of the *software is* available for checkout in the library.

Check Your Understanding of None, Any, Some, All, and Most

In each sentence, circle the correct verb enclosed in parentheses.

1. None of the e-mail message (*was, were*) deleted.

2. Some of the spectators at the game (*was, were*) hurt.

3. All of the gasoline (*has, have*) been sold.

4. None of these reports (*is, are*) ready.

5. All of the women (*has, have*) taken mathematics.

6. Most of the laser printers (*was, were*) shipped directly from the factory.

6d *The* Number and *a* Number

The number always takes a singular verb. *A* number always takes a plural verb.

> *The* number of employees *is* increasing.
> *A* number of people *have* not answered the questionnaire.

Check Your Understanding of *the* Number and *a* Number

In each sentence, circle the correct verb enclosed in parentheses.

1. A number of women (*was*, *were*) working on the project.

2. The number of men present (*was*, *were*) small.

3. The number of members in our association (*was*, *were*) only ten.

4. A number of campaigns (*was*, *were*) about serious issues.

Answers: 1. were 2. was 3. was 4. were

6e *Who* and *That* Clauses

Who and *that* take verbs that agree with their antecedents. The first set of examples demonstrates the use of *who*.

> Lisa is one of those *employees* who *finish* their work.
> Joel is one of those *players* who *are* always late.
> Ms. Harney is one of those *administrators* who *write* good reports.

The important thing to remember is that *who* stands for *employees* and for *players* and for *administrators*, not for *one*. The following examples demonstrate the use of *that*.

> It was one of the most interesting *stories* that *were* ever told.
> That was one of the worst *tornadoes* that *have* ever occurred.

Check Your Understanding of *Who* and *That* Clauses

In each sentence, circle the correct verb enclosed in parentheses.

1. Anne is among the subscribers who (*reads*, *read*) every book.

2. That is one of the most difficult problems that (*has*, *have*) ever been presented to me.

3. Aaron is one of the kindest presidents who (*has*, *have*) ever headed a company.

4. Audrey is one of the best workers who (*has*, *have*) been employed in the school department.

5. Leslie is the one person who never (*charges*, *charge*) for overtime.

Answers. 1. read 2. have 3. have 4. have 5. charges

Increasing Vocabulary

In each sentence, cross out any verb used incorrectly, and write the correct form above it. If there is no error in the sentence, write correct after it. Three sentences are incorrect.

1. The number of words in the English language is over 600,000.

2. This news, useful for success in life, appear in many articles.

3. *Four Ways to Increase Your Vocabulary* is a valuable reference.

4. A number of students was using crossword puzzles to increase vocabulary.

5. Twenty dollars, in fact, is the correct price for the speed-reading course.

6. Penny is one of those students who find the vocabulary practice helpful.

7. Most of the students also find drill and practice effective.

8. The number of people seeking improvement is increasing.

9. Some of the advice includes talking to well-informed people and reading good books and magazines.

10. Most of it requires using the dictionary and finding new words.

11. Some of the new telecommunications terms have been accepted by the general public.

12. A thesaurus is one of the most useful references that is required for composition classes.

IMPROVE YOUR VOCABULARY
Prefixes and Roots

COM, CON: with, together

Com means *with* or *together* as in *con*voke, to call *together*. *Com* appears in hundreds of words, appearing in one of these forms: *co, cog, col, con,* and *cor*: *co*here, *cog*nate, *col*lect, *com*press, and *cor*relative.

> Coherent, to stick *together*; the act of sticking *together*. (*haerere*, to stick)
>
> Collaborate, to work *together*; to work together, especially in some undertaking. (*laborare*, to work)
>
> Collusion, to play *with*; a secret agreement for illegal purposes. (*ludere*, to play)
>
> Commute, to change *with*; exchange; substitute. (*mutare*, to change)
>
> Corroborate, to strengthen *together*; confirm; support. (*robur*, strength)

Examples

Together, the students were able to give a *coherent* account of what had happened.

Collaborators work *together* to produce books.

When two people play into each other's hands or scheme *together* in a fraud or deception, they are said to be in *collusion*.

Commute means to exchange a punishment *with* a less severe one.

Stanley was fortunate to have friends to *corroborate* or agree *with* his testimony.

Other words for recognizing prefixes and roots: cognate, cognizant, concentric, condescend, convivial, corrosion, and hundreds of other words.

Vocabulary Check

Match words with definitions by placing the correct letter in each blank.

_____ 1. coherent   a. to lessen the severity of
_____ 2. collaborate   b. secret and unlawful agreement
_____ 3. collusion   c. a mark or design
_____ 4. commute   d. to work together
_____ 5. corroborate   e. clear
                                         f. to confirm; agree

Pronouns

	This lesson covers pronouns.	
7a	**The subject forms of pronouns.**	*My friend and I were late.* *Who is there?*
7b	**The object forms of pronouns.**	*Between you and me, I think they are wrong. To whom did you speak?*
7c	**Self-words.**	*The dean spoke with Fred and me.* *(not myself)*
7d	**Comparisons after as or than.**	*I am smarter than she. (is)*
7e	**The possessive form with -ing words.**	*I hate his playing the drums.*

It is a simple matter to decide whether to say, "Pass the salad to John and *me* or to John and *I*." Just omit the other person or persons mentioned. You would say, "Pass the salad to *me*." For some reason, many of us are afraid to use the word *me*. In Lesson 7, you will find the practice you need for avoiding this error.

7a The Subject Forms of Pronouns

Use the subject forms of pronouns—*I*, *he*, *she*, *we*, *they*—for the subject and subject complement. The same rule applies to *who*.

> Jim and *I* decided against the expansion. (Subject)
> It was *she* who wrote the memo. (Subject complement)
> *Who* filed the accident report? (Subject)

Note: For informal speech, authorities regard "It is me" as acceptable.

Some pronouns are followed by a noun that stands for the same person or thing. In the following sentence, *we* is the true subject of the sentence and therefore requires the subject form of the pronoun.

> *Incorrect*:   *Us* students have read the newspaper.
> *Correct*:   *We* students have read the newspaper.

Check Your Understanding of the Subject Forms of Pronouns

For each sentence, circle the correct pronoun enclosed in parentheses.

1. It was (*they*, *them*).
2. (*He*, *Him*) and (*me*, *I*) are planning to build a canoe.
3. Tanya, Bob, and (*me*, *I*) were appointed delegates.
4. (*Her*, *She*) and I arrived at the same time.
5. The most dependable workers are Joey and (*I*, *me*).

Answers: 1. they **2.** He and I **3.** I **4.** She **5.** I

7b The Object Forms of Pronouns

Use the object forms of pronouns—*me*, *him*, *her*, *us*, *them*—after action verbs and after prepositions. The same rule applies to *whom*.

> The vice president called my associate and *me*. (Direct object)
> The manager sent the agenda to *him*. (Object of the preposition)
> To *whom* did you write? (Object of the preposition)

Use the object form of the pronoun for a noun standing for the same person or thing if the noun is an object.

> *Incorrect*:   Brad insisted upon going with *we* employees.
> *Correct*:   Brad insisted upon going with *us* employees.

Step 1. Insert at the first possible point the word *he* or *him* or *she* or *her* or *they* or *them*.

Step 2. If you have inserted *he* or *she* or *they*, use *who*. If you have inserted *him* or *her* or *them*, use *whom*.

<u>Who/whom</u> did you say called?
Did you say *she* called? (who)
Who did you say called?

<u>Who/whom</u> do you wish to see?
Do you wish to see *him*? (whom)
Whom do you wish to see?

Note: The same tip can apply to the use of *who* or *whom* in subordinate clauses. Follow the same guidelines. The only difference is that *who* comes in the middle of the sentence.

Ryan is a student who/whom everybody likes.
Ryan is a student/everybody likes him. (whom)

Check Your Understanding of the Object Forms of Verbs

In each sentence, circle the correct pronoun enclosed in parentheses.

1. The human resources director called Janet and (*I*, *me*).

2. For (*who*, *whom*) did you plan the meeting?

3. We took the memo to Jamal and (*he*, *him*).

4. (*Who*, *Whom*) did you see at the conference?

5. What do you want (*we*, *us*) students to do?

Answers. 1. me 2. whom 3. him 4. Whom 5. us

Note: Use *who* for persons. Use *that* to refer to things and *which* to refer to anything except persons.

The person *who* sent me the software is Alma's friend.
A sentence *that* asks a question should end with a question mark.
The errors, *which* were minor, took a long time to correct.

7c Self-Words

Self-words are words ending in *self* or *selves*. These are *myself, your-self, himself, herself, itself, ourselves, yourselves,* and *themselves.*

A common error is to use a self-word as a subject or an object. This happens when a person tries to avoid using such pronouns as *I*.

Incorrect:	My associate and *myself* will attend.
Correct:	My associate and *I* will attend.
Incorrect:	The waiter gave the bills to Kevin and *myself.*
Correct:	The waiter gave the bills to Kevin and *me.*
Incorrect:	The tickets are for the Yengels and *ourselves.*
Correct:	The tickets are for the Yengels and *us.*

Check Your Understanding of Self-Words

In each sentence, circle the correct pronoun enclosed in parentheses.

1. The designer and (*I, myself*) arrived first.

2. The treasurer and (*I, myself*) checked the accounts.

3. The CEO gave gifts to Dorothy and (*me, myself*).

4. My wife and (*I, myself*) appreciate your courtesy.

5. The reference manuals were for (*them, themselves*).

Answers. 1. I 2. I 3. me 4. I 5. them

7d Comparisons After *As* or *Than*

Use the subject forms of the pronoun for most comparisons after *as* or *than*. The subject pronoun is the subject of the understood verb. Supply the missing verb in these sentences:

Henry is older than Elizabeth. (is)
You do not speak as well as Richard. (does)
Andrea keeps the books as well as I. (do)
Shelly and Kiko are better public speakers than Carmella and Morris. (are)

Check Your Understanding of Comparisons After *As* or *Than*

In each sentence, circle the correct pronoun enclosed in parentheses.

1. Few students can program as well as (*she*, *her*).

2. Luis is more expert in the subject than (*I*, *me*).

3. Mr. Cabrera works as hard as (*I*, *me*).

4. Were you as frightened as (*he*, *him*)?

5. She is more proficient at keyboarding than (*they*, *them*).

Answers: 1. she **2.** I **3.** I **4.** he **5.** they

7e The Possessive Form with *-ing* Words

When you are interested mainly in the action and not the person, use the possessive form of the noun or pronoun before the *gerund*, a verbal noun ending in *-ing*.

> We did not like *Mark's* (not Mark) delaying so long.
> I did not think of *his* (not him) coming so soon.
> The director objected to *my* (not me) going.

Sentence 1 does not mean that you do not like Mark. Sentence 2 does not mean that you did not think of *him*; you are mainly interested in his coming soon. Sentence 3 does not mean that the director objected to *me* but rather to my *going*. Notice that in each of these sentences the possessive form precedes a word ending with *-ing*, a gerund.

Check Your Understanding of the Possessive Form with *-ing* Words

In each sentence, circle the correct pronoun enclosed in parentheses.

1. We enjoyed (*you*, *your*) entertaining us.

2. What do you think of (*his*, *him*) going to the meeting?

3. Have you any doubt of (*Bill*, *Bill's*) arriving on time?

4. The committee insisted on (*me*, *my*) working late.

5. Have you heard of my (*sister*, *sister's*) winning the contest?

6. Do you approve of (*us*, *our*) naming your successor?

7. The supervisor approved (*my*, *me*) designing the proposed office reorganization.

Answers: 1. your **2.** his **3.** Bill's **4.** my **5.** sister's **6.** our **7.** my

Apply It !

For each sentence, supply the correct pronoun—I or me.

1. The English class is traveling to Russia with Regina and _____.

2. Ellen, Eugene, and _____ were appointed tutors.

3. The loud explosion did not frighten my friend and _____.

4. No one signed up for the Saturday class except Paul and _____.

5. June and _____ arrived at the dormitory at the same time.

6. David sent my friend and _____ two tickets to the homecoming game.

7. The testing schedule was sent to my classmates and _____.

8. The debating club sent Grace and _____ a book.

9. The lecturer gave the instructor and _____ a copy of the speech.

10. The librarian and _____ made the decision.

For each sentence, supply the correct pronoun—I, my, or me.

11. The instructor objected to _____ inability to complete the assignments on time.

12. The academic awards went to Marilyn and _____.

13. Few students can keyboard as accurately as _____.

14. Do you approve of _____ representing the college at the upcoming debate?

15. Neither Craig nor _____ was able to eliminate the computer virus.

IMPROVE YOUR VOCABULARY
Prefixes and Roots

Contra means *against*: *contra*dict, to speak against. This prefix is sometimes changed to *counter* as in *counter*act.

Contraband, *against* regulations. (*band*, band)
Contradict, to speak *against*; speak the opposite or against something. (*dicere*, to speak)
Contravene, to come *against*; to go against. (*venire*, to come)
Controversy, to turn *against*; opposition by words; a dispute. (*vertere*, turn)
Countermand, to command *against*; revoke or go against an order. (*mandare*, command)

Examples

When smugglers bring *contraband* goods into a country, they do so *against* the proclamation of the government.

A person who *contradicts* may "speak *against*" those in authority.

The smugglers *contravened*, or went *against* the law.

In a *controversy*, two or more persons argue *against* each other.

To *countermand* an order is to give an order *opposite* to what had been given.

Other words for recognizing prefixes and roots: contretemps, incontrovertible.

Vocabulary Check

Match words with definitions by placing the correct letter in each blank.

_____	1. contraband	a. to obstruct; go against the law
_____	2. contradict	b. illegal goods
_____	3. contravene	c. debate or argument; a dispute
_____	4. controversy	d. polite, affable
_____	5. countermand	e. to change or revoke an order
		f. to argue against the truth of someone's statement

Lesson ⑧

Verbs

This lesson covers

8a	*If* (and *wish*) clauses.	*If I <u>were</u> you, I would not go. I wish I <u>were</u> wealthy.*
8b	**The correct forms of certain verbs.**	*Yesterday in bed I <u>lay</u>.*
8c	**Double negatives.**	*I haven't <u>any</u> time (not <u>no</u> time).*

In Lessons 5, 6, and 7, you learned agreement and pronoun rules. In Lesson 8, you will learn the "If I *were* you" rule as well as correct forms of certain verbs. After Lesson 8, only two grammar lessons remain.

8a *If* (and *Wish*) Clauses

If the statement is a fact, use *was*. If it is not a fact or if you are uncertain *about it*, use *were*. In a statement expressing a wish, use *were*.

> If Jenny *was* ill (and she was ill), why didn't she say so?
> If I *were* you, I would refuse. (Contrary to fact)
> I wish it *were* not true. (Expressing a wish)

In the first sentence, *were* would be incorrect because it does not express a condition contrary to fact. In fact, she *was* ill.

Check Your Understanding of *If* and *Wish* Clauses

In each sentence, underline the correct verb form enclosed in parentheses.

1. If I (*was*, *were*) you, I would go to the office.

2. I wish I (*was*, *were*) the president of the company.

3. The software could be updated if it (*was*, *were*) necessary.

4. If Mr. Fisher (*was*, *were*) wealthy, he would invest his money.

5. If Alia (*was*, *were*) sure of the facts (and she was sure), she should have said so.

6. I wish I (*was*, *were*) in Florida.

7. If Blair (*was*, *were*) in town, we could start the program.

Answers. 1. were 2. were 3. were 4. were 5. was 6. were 7. were

Note: Occasionally someone says "He don't" instead of "He doesn't." Since it is wrong to say "He do not," only "He doesn't" is permitted.

8b The Correct Forms of Certain Verbs

A list of several problem verbs is included. Study them until you have memorized the ones that cause you difficulty. If you are unsure about others, use the dictionary to check on them.

Today I	Yesterday I	I have, had
arise	arose	arisen
bear	bore	borne
begin	began	begun
break	broke	broken
choose	chose	chosen
dream	dreamed or dreamt	dreamed or dreamt
drink	drank	drunk
eat	ate	eaten
forget	forgot	forgotten
get	got	got or gotten
hang (*to suspend*)	hung	hung
hang (*to put to death*)	hanged	hanged
lay	laid	laid
lie (*to recline*)	lay	lain
lead (*led*)	led	led
set (*to place an object*)	set	set

Lie and *lay* are probably the most troublesome of all verbs. *Lie* means *to rest* or *recline*. It does not take an object. *Lay* means *to place or put*. It does take an object.

Many cities *lie* along the course of a river. (No object)
I always *lay* my glasses on the desk. (Object)
The keyboard *lies* on my workstation. (No object)
Luigi *lays* carpets for the new company. (Object)

The principal parts of the two verbs follow:

	Present	*Past*	*-ing form*	*Have, has, had*
To recline	lie	lay	lying	lain
To place	lay	laid	laying	laid

Here are sentences with the principal parts of the verb *lie*. Notice that the sentences do not have objects.

She *lies* down every day.   Marilyn is *lying* down.
I *lay* down yesterday.   I *had* just *lain* down when you called.

The following are sentences with the principal parts of the verb *lay*. These sentences *do* have objects.

Nico *lays* the briefcase there each night.
I *laid* the money on the table.
They are *laying* the cornerstone now.
He has *laid* bricks in the past.

Do not think that *lie* applies only to persons. Use *lie* for inanimate (non-living) objects also.

The *branch lay* across the road.   Your *coat is lying* on the chair.

Check Your Understanding of the Correct Forms of Certain Verbs
In each sentence, circle the correct verb form enclosed in parentheses.

1. Juan (*sat*, *set*) at the computer all afternoon.

2. June (*lay*, *laid*) on the beach all yesterday afternoon.

3. I had just (*lain*, *laid*) down when the phone rang.

4. The blame (*lies*, *lays*) with you.

5. They have (*laid*, *lain*) the foundation for the new science building.

6. (*Lie*, *Lay*) down, and try to get some rest.

7. The disk is (*lying*, *laying*) where I had left it last week.

8. The guitarist has (*lead*, *led*) a fascinating life.

9. Where did you (*lay*, *lie*) that printout?

8c Double Negatives

Two negatives make an affirmative. If you say, "I haven't no time," you are saying that you have *some* time. You are not likely to write or hear such expressions, but you should avoid less obviously incorrect expressions.

Incorrect:	I won't keep you but a minute. (*Won't* and *but* are two negatives.)
Correct:	I will keep you but a minute.

Check Your Understanding of Double Negatives

Write C after the sentence if it is correct. If incorrect, cross out the incorrect word and replace with the correct word.

1. We have barely paid for our television.

2. I can hardly hear the lab assistant.

3. No one never gave me a keyboard and mouse.

4. I haven't but one car.

5. There isn't but one woman on the committee.

6. Nobody can say that I don't work hard.

7. No one ever gave me tacos for breakfast.

8. I haven't no money.

9. The interruption will last but a minute.

10. Do not give this computer to nobody.

Apply It !

Cross out two verbs used incorrectly, and write the correct forms above them.

June White was just looking to buy a new headboard for her bed when she strolled into a store near her home in White Plains, New York. She was there with her husband and children, she said, when they started trying out mattresses just for the fun of it. "My husband laid down on one of them and just said to the salesperson, 'I want this bed,'" she recalls, laughing. "When I lay on it, I couldn't get up. It was so nice, like lying on a cloud."

They bought it that day. They did not know that they had joined one of the fastest-growing home trends—foam. Several years ago, all the mattresses were made with a framework of metal innersprings surrounded by a layer of foam. Today, more mattresses are made entirely of foam. Such mattresses are not cheap, most costing at least $1,000. That is why June whispered that she wished that she was wealthy.

IMPROVE YOUR VOCABULARY
Prefixes and Roots

DE: from, down

De generally means *from, down,* or *away*: *deduce,* to draw from; *debase,* to bring down; *depredate,* to make away with.

*De*ciduous, falling *down*; falling or liable to fall; not perennial or permanent. (*cadere,* to fall)

*De*crepit, to creak "*down*"; broken down, especially by age. (*crepare,* to creak)

*De*preciate, to go *down* in price; to lessen in value. (*pretium,* price)

*De*predation, to rob *from*; a robbing or plundering. (*praedare,* to plunder)

*De*rogate, to "ask *from*"; to detract or disparage. (*rogare,* to ask)

Examples

The leaves of *deciduous* trees fall off or *down* in winter.

The *decrepit,* creaking chair was worn *down* from long use.

If a car *depreciates,* the price goes *down.*

The *derogatory* remarks, which took away *from* his good name, irritated him.

His great estate was liable to *depredation,* a plundering or robbing *from.*

Other words for recognizing prefixes and roots: dejected, demented, denote, depose.

Vocabulary Check

Match words with definitions by placing the correct letter in each blank.

_____ 1. deciduous   a. feeble from age or disease

_____ 2. decrepit   b. laying waste; plundering

_____ 3. depreciates   c. tending to belittle or degrade

_____ 4. depredation   d. to fall in value

_____ 5. derogatory   e. having leaves that fall off every year

                       f. to recognize clearly

Adjectives and Adverbs

	This lesson covers adjectives and adverbs.	
9a	Adjectives and adverbs.	Sunil does his work <u>well</u>.
9b	The articles *a* and *an*.	<u>A</u> year had gone by. <u>An</u> uncle presented the gift.
9c	Comparing two or more adjectives or adverbs.	This is the <u>better</u> of the two. This is the <u>best</u> of the three.
9d	*This, that, these,* and *those.*	<u>This</u> kind of envelope will not do. <u>These</u> types of errors should be corrected.

Should you say "*a* honor" or "*an* honor"? *An* honor is correct—and for the simple reason that it sounds better. In Lesson 9, you will also learn about choosing the right adjective, such as *better* or *best*, and using *this* or *these* correctly.

9a Adjectives and Adverbs

To avoid such errors as "I feel *badly*," follow these guidelines:

1. When the words *feel, look, smell, sound, taste, become, seem, remain,* and the like *do not express action*, omit the *ly*, and use the adjective. Pay particular attention to the verbs *feel* and *look*.

    She feels *bad*.   They look *bad*.

2. Use the *ly* form of a word—the adverb—if the verb expresses action. Use it also if it modifies an adjective or another adverb.

    Mia works *rapidly*. (*Rapidly* describes the action verb *works*.)
    Her work is *exceptionally* good. (*Exceptionally* describes the adjective *good*.)
    Jordan wrote *really* quickly. (*Really* describes the adverb *quickly*.)

Well can be used either as an adverb or as an adjective. Use *well* as an adverb to describe an action. Use *well* as an adjective only to describe a state of good health.

    The author writes *well*.   The patient feels *well*.

Which is correct? Go *slow*? Or go *slowly*? Either is correct. Since *go* expresses action, *ly* might sound better.

Check Your Understanding of Adjectives and Adverbs

In each sentence, circle the correct adjective or adverb enclosed in parentheses.

1. Rosanna is very competent; in fact, she is (*real, really*) brilliant.

2. Employees have to do things (*good, well*).

3. Because of her recent cold, she did not feel (*good, well*).

4. Raymond speaks too (*quick, quickly*).

5. I am (*real, really*) glad to find out about the merger.

6. Leslie felt (*bad, badly*) about her associate's demotion.

7. Always play the game (*fair, fairly*).

8. That Mexican dish tastes (*well, good*).

9. Ethan spoke as (*distinct*, *distinctly*) as he could.

10. Can you speak Spanish as (*good*, *well*) as you speak English?

Answers. 1. really 2. well 3. well 4. quickly 5. really 6. bad 7. fairly 8. good 9. distinctly 10. well

9b The Articles *A* and *An*

The choice between *a* or *an* is determined by *sound*. Generally, *an* is used before a vowel sound and *a* is used before a consonant *sound*, including long <u>u</u> (as in <u>use</u>). For the word historical, some controversy exists because the *h* is not silent. For this text, however, *an* historical document is preferred.

a hint	*a* university	*a* mistake
an article	*an* honor	*an* enchilada

an orange, *an* apple, and *a* pear are on the table.
a union, *a* utility, and *a* unit have sounds in common.

Check Your Understanding of the Articles *A* and *An*
Circle the adjective or adverb in the parentheses.

1. It appears that there is (*a*, *an*) increase in cost.

2. It was (*a*, *an*) honest mistake.

3. She could not find (*a*, *an*) blank disk.

4. Jan was a member of (*a*, *an*) historical society.

5. Brandon was (*a*, *an*) hero to all.

6. (*A*, *An*) mistake had been made.

Answers. 1. an 2. an 3. an 4. a or an 5. a 6. A

9c Comparing Two or More Adjectives or Adverbs
The comparison of adjectives is the variation by which they express different degrees or qualities.

Adjectives

A	B	C
One	*Two*	*More Than Two*
tall	taller	tallest
good	better	best
beautiful	more beautiful	most beautiful

Use the words in Column A (positive degree) when simply *describing* and not comparing an object with any other or others.

John is a *good* student.

In comparing *two* objects, always use words from Column B (comparative degree).

John is *older* than Joanne. (Two persons are compared.)

In comparing *more than two* objects, use the words from Column C (superlative degree).

John is the *oldest* student in his class. (More than two are compared.)

For two persons or things, adjectives of one syllable are commonly formed by adding *r* or *er* to the positive (wise, wiser) and the superlative by adding *st* or *est* (wisest). Adjectives of more than one syllable are generally compared by prefixing *more* and *most* to the positive (generous, more generous, most generous).

Adverbs

Like adjectives, many adverbs can be compared. Most of those ending in *ly* are compared by *more* and *most*. A few are compared by adding *er* and *est* (soon, sooner, and soonest). The following are compared irregularly:

A	B	C
One	*Two*	*More Than Two*
fast	faster	fastest
well	better	best
quietly	more quietly	most quietly

Use words in Column A (positive degree) when merely *describing* and not comparing an article with any other or others.

Kelsey writes forcefully.

When comparing *two* items, use the words in Column B (comparative degree).

Joshua writes *more* forcefully than Kelsey. (Two persons are compared.)

When comparing *more than two* items, use the words in Column C (superlative degree).

> Of the three, Brian writes the *most* forcefully. (More than two are compared.)

Check Your Understanding of Adjectives or Adverbs

In each sentence, circle the correct adjective or adverb enclosed in parentheses.

1. Who is the (*better*, *best*) writer—James or Joanne?

2. January was the (*colder*, *coldest*) month of the year.

3. The two positions are challenging, but the managerial one is the (*more*, *most*) interesting.

4. Of the two accountants, he is the (*least*, *less*) capable.

5. Of all his courses, Zoey found cost accounting the (*more*, *most*) practical.

6. This is the (*greatest*, *greater*) job opportunity of the two.

7. Which is the (*larger*, *largest*) state—California or New Mexico?

8. Of the three sets of glasses, these are the (*better*, *best*).

9. Derrick keyed more (*accurate*, *accurately*) than either Bob or Ivana.

Answers. 1. better 2. coldest 3. more 4. less 5. most 6. greater 7. larger 8. best 9. accurately

9d *This, That, These,* and *Those*

Although there is nothing difficult about the use of these words, few persons use them correctly. Remember: *This* and *that* refer to one thing. *These* and *those* refer to more than one.

> I do not like *this* kind of paper. (One)
> What do you think of *these* kinds of credit cards? (More than one)

Check Your Understanding of This, That, These, and Those

In each sentence, circle the correct form from the choices given in parentheses.

1. We have only (*that*, *those*) kinds of ink cartridges.

2. I prefer (*this*, *these*) kind of writing paper.

3. He did not order (*that, those)* kind of wireless mouse.

4. They did not like (*this, these*) kind of surprise exams.

5. (*That, Those*) kinds of study guides are most helpful.

6. (*This, These*) kind of lemon dessert is tart.

7. What do you think of (*that, those*) kind of accidental injury insurance?

8. I like (*this, these*) kinds of vegetables.

9. (*This, these*) kind of spelling error is inexcusable.

10. I never saw (*this, these*) sort of quiz question before.

Answers. 1. those 2. this 3. that 4. this 5. Those 6. This 7. that 8. these 9. This 10. this

Patience

Cross out the adjective or adverb used incorrectly, and write the correct form above it. Find four errors.

The researchers found an article on the virtue of patience. These kind of document is not usually real clear or well written, but this one is the best of the two found previously. It reads, "Patience comforts the poor and moderates the rich; it makes us humble in prosperity, cheerful in adversity, and unmoved by calumny."

The researchers concluded that patience, which means the capacity for calm or endurance, is the better of the three character traits they investigated.

Note: *Calumny* is a false statement maliciously made to injure someone.

IMPROVE YOUR VOCABULARY
Prefixes and Roots

DIS: apart, not

Dis generally implies *separation* or *disunion* as in dissolve. *Dis* sometimes has a negative use as in *dis*approve. *Dis* also takes the forms *di* and *dif* as in *di*verge, *dif*fuse.

> Discern, to separate *apart*; to recognize clearly. (*cernere*, to separate)
> Disparity, *not* equal; unequal. (*par*, equal)
> Dispute, to think *apart*; argue; debate. (*putare*, to think)
> Disquisition, to seek *apart*; a formal discussion. (*quarere*, to seek)
> Dissonance, a sound *apart*; any lack of harmony. (*sonus*, a sound)

Examples

To *discern* is to distinguish something *apart* from its surroundings or background.

A *disparity* in the ages of two children indicates that they were *not* equal in years.

To *dispute* is to oppose another in argument—to go *apart* or in the opposite direction.

A *disquisition* is a formal inquiry into a subject, a seeking *apart* of information.

Something is *dissonant* when it is unpleasant to the ear or *apart* from harmony.

Other words for recognizing prefixes and roots: diffident, disembark, disputation, diversity.

Vocabulary Check

Match words with definitions by placing the correct letter in each blank.

_____ 1. discern   a. a breaking up into parts
_____ 2. disparity   b. a formal discussion
_____ 3. dispute   c. to distinguish mentally; to judge
_____ 4. disquisition   d. to debate; argue
_____ 5. dissonant   e. inequality of station, rank, degree, or excellence
           f. inharmonious

Prepositions

This lesson covers prepositions.

10a	Errors in the use of prepositions.	The <u>two</u> divided the money <u>between</u> them. The money was divided <u>among</u> the <u>five</u> heirs.
10b	Special prepositions with certain words.	Ray was angry <u>with</u> his friend. This lesson is different <u>from</u> that lesson.

Do you know that you should generally use *between* when referring to two objects and *among* when referring to more than two? And did you know that it is incorrect to say, "Kristen acts *like* she will win the contest," but correct to say "Kristen acts *as if* she will win." This lesson presents guidelines and practice to help you follow these and other rules.

10a Errors in the Use of Prepositions

Many of the common prepositions are often used incorrectly. Since a preposition expresses a relationship between the object and some other word in the sentence, the preposition you use must be selected with care. Here are some ways in which you can avoid making errors with prepositions:

Between, Among

Between is considered correct for two objects but may be used for more than two when each object is considered in its relationship to others.

> The two brothers discussed the problem *between* them.
> We divided the assignment *between* Larry and Stephanie.
> The fruit trees have enough space *between* them.
> The treaty *between* the five countries was signed.

When more than two objects are spoken of collectively, however, *among* is the proper word.

> The five winners divided the money *among* themselves.
> They distributed the candy *among* the six children.
> The three students settled the dispute *among* themselves.
> The questionnaires were circulated *among* the guests.

Of

Of should not be used in place of *have*.

> We should *have* gone to the convention. (Not *of*)
> Ivan must *have* taken it. (Not *of*)

Beside, Besides

Beside is used as a preposition meaning "at the side of." *Besides* is used as an adverb and means "in addition."

> The teacher placed the chair *beside* the desk. (Preposition)
> *Besides*, the expense for the vacation is too high. (Adverb)

Due to

Due to should be avoided as a prepositional phrase. *Because of* is preferred.

> *Original*:   *Due to* a misunderstanding, I did not meet him.
> *Preferred*:   *Because of* a misunderstanding, I did not meet him.

Like, As

"The instruments looked *like* Dr. Parks had created them herself" should read, "The instruments looked *as if* Dr. Parks had created them herself." The problem is that the writer used the preposition *like* as a conjunction; a preposition can have only a noun or pronoun as its object, not a clause.

Incorrect:	The office looks *like* it had been ransacked.
Correct:	The office looks *as if* it had been ransacked.

Off of

Do not use extra prepositions such as *off of* for *off*. The *of* should not be added. Omit other unnecessary prepositions, such as the *to* in "Where is he going *to*?"

Incorrect:	The diver jumped *off of* the pier.
Correct:	The diver jumped *off* the pier.

In, Into

The preposition *in* indicates location or motion within a place. *Into* indicates motion *toward the inside* of a place from the outside.

The meeting was held *in* the conference room. (Within a place)
The swimmer jumped *into* the pool. (From the outside)

Check Your Understanding of Errors in the Use of Prepositions

In each sentence, circle the correct word form enclosed in parentheses.

1. If you had wished to go there, you should (*have*, *of*) told us.

2. The new employee fell (*off of*, *off*) the ladder.

3. The messenger stepped (*into*, *in*) the room.

4. There were only two applicants (*beside*, *besides*) David.

5. Ashley sat (*beside*, *besides*) her teacher.

6. (*Among*, *Between*) you and me, there can be no misunderstanding.

7. (*Due to*, *Because of*) the accident the train had to be rerouted.

8. I plan to write the letter (*as*, *like*) you advised.

9. Cliff acts (*like*, *as if*) he were pleased, but I think he is discouraged.

10. Jim fell (*off of*, *off*) the top step.

Answers: 1. have 2. off 3. into 4. besides 5. beside 6. Between 7. Because of 8. as 9. as if 10. off

10b Special Prepositions with Certain Words

Many words take a certain preposition for a certain meaning. Dictionaries often give the preposition required, but studying this lesson can also help. Some of these words follow:

Agree to, Agree With

One agrees *to* a proposal but agrees *with* a person.

> The manager agreed *to* my proposal.
> The members *agree with* the president.

Angry With, Angry at

One becomes *angry with* a person but *angry at* a situation.

> Janet became *angry with* the members of the council.
> Hector was *angry at* the long delay.

Differ With, Differ From

Differ with means to disagree with someone. *Differ from* means to be dissimilar.

> I *differ with* you about her eligibility.
> Maine *differs from* New Hampshire in many ways.

Different From, Different Than

The accepted form is *different from*, not *different than*. This common error can be avoided by remembering that the word "from" is a preposition and the word "than" a conjunction.

> *Incorrect*: This keyboard is different *than* that keyboard.
> *Correct*: This keyboard is different *from* that keyboard.

The less formal *different than*, however, is accepted by some authorities if the expression is followed by a clause as in the following example:

> *Acceptable*: The play was somewhat different *than* what I had expected.
> *Preferred*: The play was somewhat different *from* what I had expected.

Try to

Try to is correctly used. The verb *try* should be followed by *to*, not by *and*.

> *Incorrect*: Please try *and* be on time tomorrow.
> *Correct*: Please try *to* be on time tomorrow.

Check Your Understanding of Special Prepositions with Certain Words

For each sentence, circle the correct word form enclosed in parentheses.

1. Your opinion is different (*from*, *than*) mine.

2. I differ (*with*, *from*) you about his qualifications.

3. I agree (*with*, *to*) your plan for saving money.

4. The movie is different (*from*, *than*) the book.

5. The accountant became angry (*at*, *with*) the condition of the files.

Answers. 1. from 2. with 3. to 4. from 5. at

Memo on Prepositions

In each sentence, cross out the word form used incorrectly, and write the correct form above it. Each of the sentences in the list needs correcting.

Apply It

TO: All Office Employees
FROM: Director of Communication
DATE: April 25, 200-
SUBJECT: Preventing Mistakes with Prepositions

In recent months, we have received letters and reports with errors in the use of prepositions. Please make sure that from now on all your department heads avoid the following errors:

1. In the future, try <u>and</u> express yourself more clearly.

2. Hunter dived <u>in</u> the water from the pier.

3. The committee differed <u>from</u> me about the plans.

4. Destiny's standards of living are different <u>than</u> yours.

5. The manager has agreed <u>with</u> my proposition.

6. The work should be divided <u>between</u> the three consultants.

7. The notice said the employees should <u>of</u> attended the meeting.

8. Please keep <u>off of</u> the grass.

9. The workers are angry <u>at</u> the sales manager.

10. This workstation is different <u>than</u> that workstation.

IMPROVE YOUR VOCABULARY
Prefixes and Roots

E, EX: out, out of, away from

E or *ex* means *out*, *out of*, or *from* as in *e*ject, to cast out and *e*vade, to escape from. This prefix also takes the forms *ec* and *ef* as in *ec*centric, *ef*face.

> Excavate, to hollow *out*. (*cavus*, hollow)
> Exceed, to go beyond or *away from* a limit. (*cedere*, to go)
> Exclude, to close *out*. (*claudere*, to close)
> Expand, to spread *out*. (*pandere*, to spread)
> Extenuate, to thin *out*; to make something seem less serious.
>   (*tenuis*, thin)

Examples

When the site was *excavated*, the earth was dug *away from* it.

To *exceed* the speed limit is to go *out of* the proper range of speed.

If one is *excluded* from a social gathering, one is shut *out* of it.

To *expand* is to spread *out*.

The judge maintained that circumstances did not *extenuate*—diminish or thin *out*—the crime.

Other words for recognizing prefixes and roots: emerge, exacerbate, exasperate, excerpt, excoriate, exonerate, expurgate, extol, extort, extract.

Vocabulary Check

Match words with definitions by placing the correct letter in each blank.

_____ 1. excavate	a. to make thin; to lessen
_____ 2. exceed	b. to increase in size
_____ 3. exclude	c. to shut out
_____ 4. expand	d. to caution
_____ 5. extenuate	e. to excel; to go beyond
	f. to hollow out; cut into

Lesson (11)

Grammar Practice

This lesson is a check-up of grammar elements you've learned so far.

Pronouns

Subjects and verbs

Adjectives and adverbs

Prepositions

It is not enough to be able to answer correctly once or even several times. You must be able to answer automatically or almost without thinking. Lesson 11 will help you do this by having you make your responses become a habit. Be sure, then, to follow these guidelines:

1. Do the exercises orally. <u>Do not mark the sentence itself</u>. Instead, write the answers on a sheet of paper. This makes it possible for you to repeat the practices until you can answer automatically.

2. The answers are at the end of the lesson, so be sure to check them as needed.

3. Continue to do each practice until you respond not only correctly but without hesitation—<u>until answering correctly becomes a habit</u>.

83

Exercise 1

Choose the pronoun enclosed in parentheses that would make the sentence correct. (Reminder: <u>Do not mark the sentence itself</u>.)

1. The personnel manager called Robin and (*I, me*).
2. Ted, Jean, and (*I, myself*) were hired for the position.
3. They spoke to George and (*I, me*).
4. To (*who, whom*) did you give the performance appraisal?
5. Paula and (*I, me*) sent the invitations.
6. Kyle gave the books to my friend and (*myself, me*).
7. Kaitlyn and (*I, me*) signed the certificate.
8. Please bring Ella and (*I, me*) to the meeting.
9. Please call my associate or (*I, me*).
10. They intended the software for Sarah and (*I, me*).

Exercise 2

Choose the verb enclosed in parentheses that would make the sentence correct.

1. The meaning of the directions (*is, are*) unclear.
2. A box of compact disks (*was, were*) delivered today.
3. That collection of papers (*is, are*) valuable.
4. The applications of this rule (*vary, varies*).
5. The use of these devices (*has, have*) reduced our expenses.
6. The merger of the companies (*was, were*) not complete.
7. Part of the order (*has, have*) been filled.
8. Opportunities for improvement (*is, are*) offered.
9. The value of these books (*is, are*) in their illustrations.
10. New methods of electronic filing (*has, have*) been introduced.

Exercise 3

Choose the adjective or adverb enclosed in parentheses that would make the sentence correct.

1. The plan is a (*real, really*) simple one.
2. The sweatshirt fits (*well, good*).
3. They played the game (*fair, fairly*).
4. Paige spoke as (*distinct, distinctly*) as she could.
5. It (*sure, surely*) is cold in this classroom.
6. He felt (*bad, badly*) about his demotion.

7. How (*clear*, *clearly*) she read your name!
8. Who is the (*better*, *best*) employee—Ryan or Mason?
9. Of all the reports, Sarah's is the (*more*, *most*) complete.
10. Which is the (*larger*, *largest*) city, Los Angeles or New York?

Exercise 4

For each sentence, choose the pronoun enclosed in parentheses that would make the sentence correct.

1. Everyone was allowed to make (*his*, *their*) decision.
2. Nobody signed (*her*, *their*) name to the petition.
3. Anyone dissatisfied may have (*his or her*, *their*) money back.
4. Several left (*his*, *their*) samples at the office.
5. What should a person do if (*he is*, *they are*) asked such a question?
6. Every alumna tries to see what is good for (*her*, *them*).
7. There (*is*, *are*) several books on word processing.
8. There (*is*, *are*) many opportunities in the field.
9. There (*was*, *were*) no errors on the report.
10. Here (*is*, *are*) the manager of the bookstore.

Exercise 5

Choose the verb enclosed in parentheses that would make the sentence correct.

1. They acted as if they (*was*, *were*) wealthy.
2. If I (*was*, *were*) you, I would give up the project.
3. If the table (*was*, *were*) an antique (and you had proof that it was), why didn't you buy it?
4. I wish it (*was*, *were*) possible to read the whole document.
5. I wish I (*was*, *were*) as tall as my sister.
6. It was (*us*, *our*) coming in late that annoyed him.
7. We appreciate (*you*, *your*) finishing the work.
8. The instructor objected to (*me*, *my*) leaving.
9. The audience was annoyed with (*Joan*, *Joan's*) playing of the song.
10. The company insisted on (*me*, *my*) taking the large office.

Exercise 6

Choose the verb enclosed in parentheses that would make the sentence correct.

1. They found the victim (*lying*, *laying*) on the road.
2. I (*lie*, *lay*) down every afternoon.
3. Do not leave your camera (*lying*, *laying*) around.

4. Do you (*lie*, *lay*) down when you come home?

5. The injured man has (*laid*, *lain*) unconscious for two hours.

6. He has (*laid*, *lain*) there for a long time.

7. He (*laid*, *lay*) the chart on the desk an hour ago.

8. The suspect (*hanged*, *hung*) himself.

9. (*Lie*, *Lay*) down, and try to get some rest.

10. Broken glass (*lay*, *laid*) on the floor.

Exercise 7

Choose the word enclosed in parentheses that would make the sentence correct.

1. Gavin looks (*like*, *as if*) he is happy.

2. Amanda claimed that she should (*of*, *have*) gone to the meeting.

3. The books were divided (*among*, *between*) the two children.

4. This screen saver is different (*than*, *from*) that screen saver.

5. Mr. Tedesco was angry (*at*, *with*) his associate.

6. The scissors (*is*, *are*) missing from the shelf.

7. None of the textbooks (*was*, *were*) missing.

8. All of the computers (*is*, *are*) new.

9. None of the food (*was*, *were*) spoiled.

10. *The Merry Wives of Windsor* (*is*, *are*) not on the reading list.

Letter of Application

Find the errors! There are seven grammar errors in the following rough-draft letter. Make the necessary corrections by crossing out incorrect words and writing the correct forms above them.

August 22, 200-

Mr. Leland Jeffers, Managing Editor
Goodman Publishing Company
4677 Mission Street
Seattle, WA 98122

Dear Mr. Jeffers:

In response to your recent *Wall Street Journal* advertisement, I would

appreciate you considering me an applicant for Developmental Editor. As I

will explain, I believe I meet your requirements for this position.

On my own, I have assisted the Board of Trustees in their effort to

provide a program in which there are a variety of positions. Every one of

the employees have found me to be a person who never lays down on the

job. Recently my supervisor praised my associate and I for our writing ability.

She felt badly that the others did not recommend us.

IMPROVE YOUR VOCABULARY
Prefixes and Roots

Before a verb, *in* means *in*, *on*, *into*, or *against*: *in*sert, to place *in*; *in*dict, to speak *against*. Before an adjective, *in* has a negative meaning nearly equivalent to *not*: *in*active, not active; *in*secure, not secure. This prefix also takes the forms *em*, *en*, *ig*, *il*, *im*, and *ir* as in *em*boss, *en*grave, *ig*noble, *il*legal, *im*placable, and *ir*radiate.

*Il*luminate, to throw light *on*; enlighten. (*luminare*, to light)
*Im*migrant, migrate *in*; one who comes into a country. (*migrate*, to settle in another country)
*In*carcerate, to put *into* prison; imprison. (*carcer*, prison)
*In*dict, to speak *against*; charge with a crime. (*dicere*, to speak)
*In*undate, *in* plus a wave; to overflow as with a flood. (*unda*, a wave)

Examples

To *illuminate* a portrait is to throw light *on* it.

An *immigrant* is one who migrates *into* a country.

To *incarcerate* is to put *into* prison.

Indict is to charge *against* the supposed offender.

When the river overflows, it *inundates* or overspreads *into* the countryside.

Other words for recognizing prefixes and roots: incentive, indigence, intrude.

Vocabulary Check

Match words with definitions by placing the correct letter in each blank.

_____ 1. illuminate   a. to imprison
_____ 2. immigrant   b. to charge with, as a crime
_____ 3. incarcerate   c. to shed light upon
_____ 4. indict   d. ill tempered
_____ 5. inundate   e. a person who comes into a new country
                    f. to flood

*No one can write
well who does not
punctuate well.
Punctuation is as
integral and as
important a part
of what is written
as are the words.
—Arlo Bates, Talks
on Writing English*

Punctuation

Do You Make These Mistakes in Punctuation?

WRONG	RIGHT
Raquel drafted the proposal, then she presented it.	Raquel drafted the proposal. Then she presented it.
If it rains we will go home.	If it rains, we will go home.
We bought pens, paper and cards.	We bought pens, paper, and cards.
This is what the problem is, and what you should do about it.	This is what the problem is and what you should do about it.
Graduation was June 10th.	Graduation was June 10.
Boy's coats were on sale.	Boys' coats were on sale.
Part time work was available.	Part-time work was available.

"Clearness first" has always been the writer's aim. And for clearness, nothing is more important than proper punctuation. Also, good punctuation—especially a better understanding of the use of the dash, semicolon, and hyphen—can help you write more forceful sentences.

Always follow the standard rules for the comma. Some authorities suggest that it may not be necessary to use the comma in a compound sentence if the clauses are short. This is wrong. By the time you try to figure out if they are short enough, you have wasted your time—and hurt your chances for punctuating easily and automatically.

LESSON 12

PART 3 PRETEST

A one comma **B** two commas **C** no comma(s) **D** semicolon

1. If it jams_ force it. _____

2. If it breaks_ it needed replacing anyway. _____

3. Murphy claimed_ "Nothing is as easy at it looks." _____

4. In order to get a loan_ you must first prove you don't need it. _____

5. It was an important meeting_ yet few attended. _____

6. The person answering the complaint should express sympathy_ and explain how the error occurred. _____

7. Robert Louis Stevenson was born on November 13, 1850_ in Edinburgh, Scotland. _____

8. Do not put too much in a sentence_ do not put too little. _____

9. The person_ who is standing by the door_ is my friend. _____

10. I will review the spreadsheet_ then I will return it. _____

A correct **B** incorrect

11. Sharp hikes—6 percent or more—could delay recovery. _____

12. The highly-touted program was surprisingly cheap. _____

13. The taste sensations are: sweet, sour, bitter, and salt. _____

14. Jenna said, "I am going to class." _____

15. The worker forgot the power company's warning. _____

16. It is only a few minute's walk to the office. _____

17. Most summer vacations end with Labor Day. _____

18. The Senate has not voted on the issue yet. _____

19. Ten people were at the conference. _____

20. Did you buy the book "Writing to Communicate"? _____

Punctuation of the Simple Sentence

12a	**Words in a series.**	*We bought staples, paper clips, and tape.*
12b	**Adjectives in a series.**	*My sister is an honest, reliable person.*
12c	**Explanatory words (appositives).**	*Henry Girard, treasurer, is on leave.*
12d	**Parenthetical expressions.**	*The newspaper, however, is missing.*
12e	**Direct address.**	*Friends, we are meeting here for a happy occasion.*
12f	**Introductory words.**	*Well, these are the directions.*

A simple sentence consists of one independent clause. It has *one* subject and *one* predicate but may contain an indefinite number of words and phrases. If another clause is added, it becomes either a complex or compound sentence. The sentences in Lesson 12 are simple, although the rules may also apply to the complex and compound sentence.

12a Words in a Series

Use a comma between each item in a series, a series being at least three items that follow one another.

> The student asked for paper, pens, and a ruler for his project.
> For exercise, Beth walked to school, to the shops, and to business.
> A keyboard, mouse, and CPU were provided.

Omitting the comma before the *and* can sometimes make a great difference in meaning as in the following sentence:

> Mr. Randall, Mr. Soto and Mr. Hughes are waiting to see you.

This sentence with one comma could be interpreted to mean that someone was addressing Mr. Randall and that the others were waiting to see him. If the writer does not intend this meaning, the sentence should be punctuated in this way:

> Mr. Randall, Mr. Soto, and Mr. Hughes are waiting to see you.

Omit commas, however, when each item is connected by *and* or *or*.

> Try to be tactful and friendly and helpful.
> They studied and took the exam and passed it.

Check Your Understanding of Words in a Series

For each sentence, place commas where needed. If no commas are needed, write a C after the sentence.

1. The seasons are spring summer autumn and winter.

2. The qualities of style are clearness force and elegance.

3. The delivery will be made today tomorrow or Friday.

4. The glider soared and dipped and banked.

5. These were blue green and red flags.

6. They visited many cities towns and villages.

7. The price of food clothing and entertainment is rising.

8. A check or cash or money order will do.

9. My favorite authors are Stevenson Dickens and Poe.

10. The executive lays out plans assigns them to subordinates and then devotes attention to exceptions.

12b Adjectives in a Series

Separate two coordinate (equal) adjectives with a comma.

> The *efficient, trustworthy* assistant received a raise in pay.
> Nancy had the *right mental* attitude.

Use a comma only if you can place the word *and* between the two adjectives. Since "an efficient *and* trustworthy assistant" makes sense, you would use a comma in the first sentence. And since "the right *and* mental attitude" does not make sense, you would not use a comma in the second sentence.

Check Your Understanding of Adjectives in a Series

For each sentence, place commas where needed. If no commas are needed, write a C after the sentence.

1. Cynthia became an older wiser person in a short time.

2. Jim opened the large cardboard box.

3. She was an honest respected lawyer.

4. The five new computers are here.

5. Every thoughtful ambitious person voted.

6. They were courteous conscientious receptionists.

12c Explanatory Words (Appositives)

Separate appositives from the rest of the sentence.

> The author's first book, *Learning Power*, sold a million copies.
> Dr. Tucker, *the president of the college*, spoke at the event.

Most appositives are nonessential and require commas to show that they are not needed. Some appositives, however, are essential to the meaning or so commonly used that commas should not be used.

> His friend Jack was not a student last semester.
> My sister Geri has received two awards.

Check Your Understanding of Explanatory Words

For each sentence, place commas where needed. If no commas are needed, write a C after the sentence.

1. Ms. Lawler the owner of the business is a competent person.

2. Milton the English poet wrote *Paradise Lost*.

3. Ronald Nelson Director of Marketing implemented a new program.

4. They visited Fall River a great textile city of the nineteenth century.

5. Mrs. Allen our accountant is on vacation.

6. He himself wanted to hire an industrial expert.

7. Susan Bringola an employee of the company was at the meeting.

8. The rabbit a widespread, adaptable animal is able to survive almost everywhere.

Answers: 1. Lawler,/owner, 2. Milton,/poet, 3. Nelson,/Marketing, 4. River,/city, 5. Mrs. Allen,/accountant, 6. correct 7. Bringola,/company, 8. rabbit,/animal,

12d Parenthetical Expressions

Use a comma or commas to set off words and phrases used parenthetically.

A rule of thumb is to use a comma or commas if the word or phrase requires a pause in reading.

> *Of course* you're going. (no pause)
> This is, *of course*, a memorable occasion. (pause)

The parenthetical word or phrase, an independent element of the sentence, is not a part of the subject or predicate and is merely "thrown in." It can be introductory or can appear anywhere in the sentence.

The following words and phrases are often, though not always, used parenthetically.

Words and Phrases Often Used Parenthetically

accordingly	for example	indeed	otherwise
also	furthermore	moreover	perhaps
besides	however	now	then
consequently	in contrast	of course	therefore

In the following sentences, notice how you need to pause when reading the word surrounded with a comma or commas.

The new employee was *indeed* guilty.
Indeed, he conducted himself well in other respects.

Then I mailed the letters to the accountant.
On these facts, *then*, I rested my argument.

She has the necessary skills and will *therefore* be hired.
Your conclusion, *therefore*, has not been proved.

I have *now* shown the consistency of my argument.
Now, what is the fair and obvious conclusion?

We must pay attention, *however*, to the opinions of others.
(*However* used parenthetically always requires commas.)

Check Your Understanding of Parenthetical Expressions

For each sentence, place commas where needed. If no commas are needed, write a C after the sentence.

1. This medicine for example is harmless.

2. Enthusiasm however is a desirable quality.

3. Besides public outrage appeared to be rising.

4. They received the necessary help and will therefore go.

5. They believed of course that this was all they could do.

6. We have the required equipment and will therefore proceed as planned.

Answers 1. medicine,/example, 2. Enthusiasm, however, 3. Besides, 4. correct 5. believed,/course, 6. correct

12e Direct Address

Use a comma or commas to set off a term of direct address from the rest of the sentence.

A noun in direct address, an independent element, is not the subject of the sentence and has no connection with the verb. Use a comma or commas, therefore, to set off all nouns in direct address.

> *Mr. Ryan*, you are always on time for the meetings.
> Come here, *Linda*, and look at this address.

Here *Mr. Ryan* attracts the attention of the person addressed. If omitted, it does not change the meaning of the sentence.

Check Your Understanding of Direct Address

For each sentence, place commas where needed. If no commas are needed, write a C after the sentence.

1. Mrs. Marsh we cannot fill your order.

2. Call me Leo the next time you visit the college.

3. I hope Carol that you can go to the meeting.

4. Friends we are meeting today for a serious reason.

5. No Lauren you cannot go.

6. We count on your presenting the facts Ray.

7. Mr. Marree will interview all job applicants.

8. We know Mary Ellen that you are joking.

Answers. 1. Mrs. Marsh, 2. me, Leo, 3. hope, Carol, 4. Friends, 5. No, Lauren, 6. facts, Ray 7. correct 8. know, Mary Ellen,

12f Introductory Words

Use a comma after introductory words such as *yes, no, well,* and *why*.

> *Yes*, the supervisor did answer the letter.
> *No*, this is not the report I wanted.
> *Well*, what do you know about business laws and ethics?
> *Why*, this is a shock!

When the words *yes*, *no*, *well*, or *why* are used in a sentence, they are usually followed by a comma.

Check Your Understanding of Introductory Words

For each sentence, place commas where needed. If no commas are needed, write a C after the sentence.

1. No the date of this note is not the same as that of the other one.

2. Well the calendar probably is incorrect.

3. Yes this is an opportunity to improve the environment.

4. Why this is the same letter I had mentioned previously.

Answers. 1. No, 2. Well, 3. Yes, 4. Why,

The Power of Persuasion

The following two paragraphs have periods, capital letters, and one comma. Add eight commas.

Apply It

Many sales letters fail because they lack the important element of persuasion. Suppose for example that in your letter you gain the attention and interest of your reader explain the benefits of your product and prove its real merit. If you bring your remarks abruptly to a close and sign your name you will probably get some orders. Suppose however that instead you show your reader how your product will be of practical value.

Perhaps your readers have never thought of the matter in just that way. Your letter persuades them that your product will put dollars and cents into their pocket. Yes they are made to see the profit rather than the expense.

IMPROVE YOUR VOCABULARY
Prefixes and Roots

INTER: among, between

Inter means *among* or *between* as in *inter*vene, to come between, and in *inter*sperse, to scatter among.

> *Inter*fere, to strike *between*; to come between; to clash. (*ferire*, to strike)
> *Inter*ject, to throw *between*; interrupt with. (*jacere*, to throw)
> *Inter*lude, to fill the time *between* two events. (*ludus*, play)
> *Inter*stice, to set *between*; a crack; crevice. (*sistere*, to set)
> *Inter*val, a wall *between*; a space between things. (*vallum*, wall)

Examples

> If you *interfere* in another person's affairs, you strike *between* him and what he is doing.

> If you *interject* a remark, you throw your words *among* those of another speaker.

> An *interlude* is really an interval *between* the acts of a play.

> In a net, the *interstices* are those spaces that stand *between* the hemp or rope.

> It seemed like a long *interval between* one event and the next.

Other words for recognizing prefixes and roots: intercede, interchange, interjection, internecine, interstellar, interrupt.

Vocabulary Check

Match words with definitions by placing the correct letter in each blank.

_____ 1. interfere   a. a narrow space
_____ 2. interject   b. periodic
_____ 3. interlude   c. to get in the way of
_____ 4. interstice   d. to throw in between
_____ 5. interval   e. time or distance between
                    f. a short entertainment between acts

Punctuation of the Simple Sentence (Continued)

This lesson continues the coverage of punctuating the simple sentence.

13a	**Verbal phrases.**	*To avoid ambiguity, writers must punctuate correctly.*
13b	**Introductory Prepositional phrases.**	*With the addition of the new wing, the dormitory will be perfect.*
13c	**Dates and addresses.**	*Edna St. Vincent Millay was born on February 22, 1892, at the little sea village of Rockland, Maine.*

When you can locate the subject and verb of a sentence, you will more easily be able to place commas after introductory words, phrases, and clauses. This ability, in turn, will help make your writing clear since your readers will be able to see at a glance what your main thought is.

13a Verbal Phrases

Use a comma to set off an introductory verbal phrase or two commas for a parenthetical verbal phrase.

A verbal phrase can be recognized by its verbal—having the *-ing* or *-ed* form of a verb or the word *to* preceding a verb.

> *Speaking before the assembly*, the principal outlined her position.
> The CEO, *stunned and confused*, cancelled the event.
> *Our time being short*, we did not attend the meeting.

Having forgotten his laptop, the eager student returned.
To win the award, she worked two weeks.

If the verbal phrase is necessary to identify a particular person or thing, however, do not use commas.

The student *standing by the blackboard* is the one I mean.
They rented a spacious office *operated by the state.*

Also, do not use a comma if the verbal phrase is the subject of the sentence.

Doing nothing can be tedious.

Check Your Understanding of Using Commas with Verbal Phrases

For each sentence, place commas where needed. If no commas are needed, write a C after the sentence.

1. Being your associate I urge you to work diligently.

2. Reservations can be made space permitting until flight time.

3. To evaluate the candidate's leadership was the most important task.

4. To meet her deadline was all she wanted.

5. To help you get there the company has created new software.

6. Using a ruler she carefully drew a map of the area.

7. Surfing the Web is an easy task.

8. To be honest I cannot remember his name.

9. To be successful you should practice every day.

Answers: 1. associate, 2. made, space permitting, 3. correct 4. correct 5. there, 6. ruler, 7. correct 8. honest, 9. successful,

13b Introductory Prepositional Phrases

Use a comma after a prepositional phrase or a combination of phrases.

At the end of the fiscal year, expenses are deducted from revenues.
In response to your request, we are submitting the information.

For clearness, it is not always necessary to use a comma after a short prepositional phrase (four words or fewer). Yet you might want to consider always using a comma in order to avoid having to decide if it is necessary or not.

| Correct: | *During the summer* we have a month's vacation. |
| Correct: | *During the summer*, we have a month's vacation. |

For some constructions, however, a comma is always necessary.

In New England, weather changes are frequent.
Before the weekend, passes were given automatically.

Check Your Understanding of Using Commas for Prepositional Phrases

For each sentence, place commas where needed. If no commas are needed, write a C after the sentence.

1. With a diversified portfolio of municipal securities the company offered a steady income.

2. During the past few years many customs have changed.

3. Under the best of circumstances no one should be alone on such an occasion.

4. In the middle of the room I stumbled over a loose cable.

Answers: 1. securities, 2. years, 3. circumstances, 4. room,

13c Dates and Addresses

Use commas to set off the day or month from the year. Use commas to set off the name of the street, city, and state. Do not, however, use a comma between the state and the ZIP code.

A common error is to omit the comma after the year. If you think of the year or the day as an interrupter, you will be more likely to place a comma after it.

The proclamation was issued on *October 22, 1962*, some time ago.
The return address was *762 Seminary Road, Richmond, VA* 02817.
Robert Burns was born on *January 25, 1759*, in Scotland.

If only the month and year are used, however, commas are not necessary.

Louisa May Alcott was born in *November 1832* in Pennsylvania.

Check Your Understanding of Dates and Addresses

For each sentence, place commas where needed.

1. Babe Ruth was born on February 6 1895.

2. The contract was signed on Wednesday April 9 1974 at the hotel.

3. The address is 524 East Street Manhattan Illinois 60360.

4. On Tuesday August 13 we began our inquiry.

5. Mrs. Lopez lived at 52 Anderson Lane Omaha Nebraska.

6. Would Thursday December 11 at 3 p.m. be good?

Answers: 1. February 6, 2. Wednesday, April 9, 1974, 3. Street, Manhattan, 4. Tuesday, August 13, 5. Lane, Omaha, 6. Thursday, December 11,

Note: Use commas to set off titles, academic degrees, and other explanatory terms.

Sarah Perkins, M.D.   Robert Black, Ph.D., of England

Apply It **!**

Clearness in Business Writing

The following paragraphs lack commas—nine to be exact. Add these commas.

Business writing needs to be extraordinarily clear. For this reason the average paragraph should be short—much less than one hundred words and no more than four or five sentences. In business in fact even single-sentence paragraphs are sometimes acceptable and even effective. (A long series of two-sentence or so paragraphs on the other hand should be avoided since such a monotonous arrangement may distract the reader.)

In order for a paragraph to be clear the sentences must be in logical order. In addition words such as *however moreover* and *consequently* should be used to help the flow of sentences.

IMPROVE YOUR VOCABULARY
Prefixes and Roots

OB: against, in the way, before

Ob generally means *against* as in *ob*struct, to build against. *Ob* also takes the forms *oc*, *of*, and *op*: *oc*cur, *of*fend, and *op*pose.

Ob*noxious*, to harm *against*; very unpleasant; offensive (*noxa*, harm)

Ob*stacle*, to stand *before*; anything that stands in the way. (*stare*, to stand)

Ob*struct*, to pile *in the way of*; to block; hinder progress and the like. (*stuere*, to pile up)

Op*portune*, timed before; well-timed. (*portus*, port)

Op*press*, to press against; *to keep down* by the unjust use of authority. (*premere*, to press)

Examples

Obnoxious habits or people are harmful to or *against* others.

An *obstacle* is a barrier or impediment that stands *in the way of* progress.

Obstruct means to be *in the way of* and prevent a clear view.

An *opportunist* is one who waits for a suitable time *before* taking action.

Anything that *oppresses* pushes or presses *against* others.

Other words for recognizing prefixes and roots: objurgate, obstreperous, obtrude, opprobrium.

Vocabulary Check

Match words with definitions by placing the correct letter in each blank.

_____ 1. obnoxious   a. offensive or harmful to others
_____ 2. obstacle   b. to block or hinder
_____ 3. obstruct   c. a hindrance; an impediment
_____ 4. opportunist   d. pertaining to the eye
_____ 5. oppress   e. one who takes advantage of opportunities as they arise
    f. to crush by hardship

Punctuation of the Compound Sentence

14a	The comma in a compound sentence.	*I lost my wallet, and my dog found it.*
14b	The semicolon in a compound sentence.	*The test was easy; I am sure I passed.*
14c	The comma in a command sentence.	*Close the door, and shut the window.*

In Part 1, you learned how to recognize a sentence, the first step in avoiding the run-on sentence. In Lesson 14, you will learn how to punctuate the compound sentence, the second step in avoiding this major sentence error. A compound sentence, as you remember from Part 1, is simply two sentences joined together.

14a The Comma in a Compound Sentence

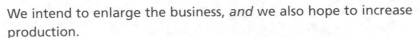

Use a comma to separate the two statements of a compound sentence only when the second statement begins with a coordinating conjunction (and, or, nor, but, yet, for, so).

> We intend to enlarge the business, *and* we also hope to increase production.
> I may consider your plan, *or* I may disregard it.
> I did not apply for the position, *nor* do I want it.
> We found the notebook, *but* the papers were not there.

I used the right key, *yet* the door would not open.

It must have been late, *for* the doors were locked.

The weather was rainy, *so* I took my umbrella.

Do not, however, use a comma with a compound predicate:

| *Incorrect*: | They performed for parents' day, and did a great job. |
| *Correct*: | They performed for parents' day and did a great job. |

The second verb, *did*, does not have its own subject. A comma would be distracting.

Note: Use the semicolon before a coordinating conjunction only if needed for clarity. (The semicolon may be used since usually the sentence already contains one or more commas.)

The dean is in Madison, Wisconsin, this week; but she will be back on Tuesday, November 21.

Check Your Understanding of the Comma in the Compound Sentence

For each sentence, place commas where needed. If no commas are needed, write a C after the sentence.

1. Alexis did not plan to go nor did she let her assistant go.

2. Edwin was an engineer but Jean was a computer expert.

3. Jonathan is an accountant and he is honest.

4. Punctuation is easy and I know I will pass the test.

5. They came to the meeting and brought the announcement.

6. The assistant was in a hurry and I therefore could not catch him.

7. Amos developed spreadsheets and used them in his work.

8. The weather looks bad yet we should not despair.

Answers: 1. go, 2. engineer, 3. accountant, 4. easy, 5. correct 6. hurry, 7. correct 8. bad,

Note: For clarity, use the semicolon to separate items in a series if the individual items contain commas.

The company opened offices in Spartanburg, South Carolina; Provo, Utah; and Pittsburgh, Pennsylvania.

14b The Semicolon in a Compound Sentence

Use a semicolon in a compound sentence when the second statement begins with any word other than a coordinating conjunction.

Even if the second statement begins with such words as *then*, *however*, and *nevertheless*, the semicolon is required. *Then* causes more difficulty than any other word.

> At first we were apprehensive; *then* we saw the humor of it.
> Marla is not here; *however*, she will be here tomorrow.
> Cody was nearly finished; *nevertheless*, he refused to leave.
> They were already late; *therefore*, they did not call ahead.
> Hurry up; *now* is the time to go.

Check Your Understanding of the Semicolon in a Compound Sentence

For each sentence, place semicolons and commas where needed. If no semicolons or commas are needed, write a C after the sentence.

1. This looks difficult however we should not give up.

2. The report is not true in fact it is false.

3. Chris opened the letter then he realized it was addressed to Tom.

4. We arrived yesterday otherwise I would have called.

5. The position on the newspaper however does not pay well.

6. The defendant had been late therefore she is trying to be attentive.

7. Mariko answered the advertisement properly thus he got the job.

Answers: 1. difficult; however, **2.** true; in fact, **3.** letter; then **4.** yesterday; otherwise, **5.** newspaper; however, **6.** late; therefore, **7.** properly; thus

14c The Comma in a Command Sentence

Use a comma with a coordinating conjunction in a command (imperative) sentence.

Remember, each command sentence really has a subject—*you*—although unexpressed. The subject *you* is understood in both clauses.

> Answer all those letters, and tell your manager that you wrote them.
> Stay with us, and do not go to New York.

Check Your Understanding of the Comma in a Command Sentence

For each sentence, place commas where needed. If no commas are needed, write a C after the sentence.

1. I was sorry to hear of your accident and hope you recuperate soon.

2. Stand quietly and speak distinctly.

3. Do not postpone the trip and do not call the press agent.

4. Lock the door and return the key.

Answers: 1. correct 2. quietly, 3. trip, 4. door,

Postponement

Two commas are already correctly placed. Place two more commas and two semicolons.

Postponement is a common fault. If you want to fail, try putting off until tomorrow what you can just as well do today. If you want to succeed on the other hand consider the value of time. There is an inexhaustible market for it. Whenever you purchase an article of value, you are buying mostly time. Manufacturers take several hundred dollars worth of materials then they turn them into expensive machines. Watchmakers buy ten dollars' worth of steel later they turn them into fine springs worth thousands of dollars. Your success depends not only on the kind of time you have to sell but on what you do with the time you have. Do not procrastinate. The road to success is paved with the good intentions of people who do not postpone anything.

IMPROVE YOUR VOCABULARY
Prefixes and Roots

Per generally means *through* as in *per*vade, to pass through or in *per*vert, to turn *by* or *from*.

Percolate, to pass *through*; filter. (*colare*, to strain)
Perennial, *through* the year; plants lasting more than two years. (*annus*, year)
Perjure, to swear *through*; swear falsely. (*jurare*, to swear)
Pernicious, to destroy *through*; causing great injury; fatal. (*necare*, to kill)
Pervert, to turn *by* or *from*; to lead astray or from a proper purpose. (*vertere*, to turn)

Examples

When coffee *percolates*, hot water passes *through* it to extract its flavor.

Perennial plants last *through* several years.

Perjury, the willful telling of a lie while under oath, is literally a swearing *through*.

Pernicious anemia is the severe form of blood disease. If not treated properly, it may be fatal, a killing "thoroughly or *through*."

Bribes *pervert* or thwart justice by turning *by* (from) it.

Other words for recognizing prefixes and roots: perceive, perfidious, perfunctory, perforate, permeate, persist, perplex, pervade.

Vocabulary Check

Match words with definitions by placing the correct letter in each blank.

_____ 1. percolate   a. a plant that lives several years
_____ 2. perennial   b. willful swearing to what is false
_____ 3. perjury   c. to turn from a proper purpose
_____ 4. pernicious   d. to annoy; irritate
_____ 5. pervert   e. to pass through a filter
                         f. highly injurious or harmful

Punctuation of the Complex Sentence

This lesson covers punctuation of the complex sentence.

15a	**Introductory clauses.**	*After the game was over, we celebrated.*
15b	***Who*** **and** ***which*** **clauses.**	*Office workers who possess these skills can succeed. Ms. White, who has these skills, is fortunate.*
15c	**Parenthetical expressions and clauses.**	*This sentence, I believe, illustrates this point.*
15d	**Direct quotations.**	*Megan announced, "I got the job!"*

A **complex sentence** is one with an independent (main) clause and one or more dependent clauses. In Lesson 15, you will see the benefit of using a comma after an introductory clause—readers can see at a glance the main thought of the sentence.

15a Introductory Clauses
Use a comma to set off an introductory clause.

Introductory clauses usually begin with words such as *after, although, as, because, before, if, since, than, though, unless, until, when, where,* and *while.*

After the contracts are signed, we will write you.
When you do not know what to do, wait.

Before we approve your loan, we must have proof of employment.
If people have no care for the future, they will soon have sorrow for the present.

No comma is usually needed if the dependent clause comes after the main one.

We can mail the videos without delay *if your order reaches us by tomorrow*.
They might not continue work *unless they find a digital camera*.

An exception is a clause introduced by *although*. Since such clauses are always unnecessary, a comma is required.

Raymond decided to accept the position, *although he was not sure he would like it.*

Punctuate elliptical sentences as if they were supplied with the omitted words. **Ellipsis** is a Greek word meaning *omission*. Compare the following sentences:

If it is possible, I will fly to Hawaii tomorrow.
If possible, I will fly to Hawaii tomorrow.

Check Your Understanding of Introductory Clauses

For each sentence, place commas where needed. If no commas are needed, write C after the sentence.

1. Since their credit rating was good they bought the beach house.

2. If you prefer you may use your password.

3. After you complete this program you will be an expert in punctuation.

4. My brother will be disappointed if I do not go.

5. If I were you I would accept the position.

6. As you probably know Aidan is our new human resources director.

7. Because the president was diligent the company succeeded.

8. If necessary they will delay their departure.

9. Learning the subject of business correspondence can be demanding.

10. What the graphic artist drew is difficult to reproduce.

Answers. 1. good, 2. prefer, 3. program, 4. correct 5. you, 6. know, 7. diligent, 8. necessary, 9. correct 10. correct

15b *Who* and *Which* Clauses

Use a comma or commas for a *who* or *which* clause when it is explanatory or presents an additional thought.

> The woman, who later proved to be a friend, seemed angry.
> Townsend, which is 50 miles away, is not on the map.

If the words *who later proved to be a friend* were omitted in the first sentence, the remaining words still mean what they were intended to mean—the woman seemed angry. In the second sentence, the same applies to Townsend even with the clause *which is 50 miles away* removed.

But omit commas for a clause necessary to identify a particular item

> Teachers must love students who are attentive and pleasant.
> The town that Rafael selected is an hour's drive.

In the first sentence, the clause *who are attentive and pleasant* is necessary to identify which students teachers must love. If removed, it changes the meaning of the sentence. In the second sentence, the clause *that Rafael selected* is necessary to identify which town is an hour's drive.

Check Your Understanding of *Who* and *Which* Clauses

For each sentence, place commas where needed. If no commas are needed, write C after the sentence.

1. My new watch which kept good time is broken.

2. The person who is standing by the door is the dean.

3. Des Moines which is the capital is the largest city in Iowa.

4. The manager who wrote the e-mail was not present.

5. Edward Droney who was offered the job is a competent worker.

6. The person who was office manager is retiring soon.

7. Vera Mason who was office manager is retiring later.

8. The new form which everyone will have to complete is causing much controversy.

Answers: 1. watch,/time, **2.** correct **3.** Des Moines,/capital, **4.** correct **5.** Droney,/job, **6.** correct **7.** Mason,/manager, **8.** form,/complete,

Note: Use a comma to prevent misunderstanding. A comma is needed for identical verbs that appear together or for a word or phrase at the beginning of a sentence that could be read incorrectly.

> What the difficulty was, was not clear.
> Ever since, weekly sales figures have been printed.

15c Parenthetical Expressions and Clauses

Use commas for parenthetical expressions that are clauses and for parenthetical clauses.

Use commas for clauses such as *I believe*, *it is certain*, and *it seems* when their position in the sentence changes from the normal order.

> I believe that the statement is in error. (Normal order)
> The statement, *I believe*, is in error. (Change from normal order)

Use commas for parenthetical clauses.

> Small companies, *if you're wondering*, are successful.
> Get a good dictionary, *authorities promise*, and you will succeed.

Check Your Understanding of Parenthetical Expressions and Clauses

For each sentence, place commas where needed.

1. Employee morale though it is difficult to define contributes to a company's success.

2. Nancy it seems almost certain continued to spend money.

3. This medicine I assure you is harmless.

4. To believe that statement is we think an error.

Answers: 1. morale,/define, 2. Nancy,/certain, 3. medicine,/you, 4. is,/think,

15d Direct Quotations

Use a comma to separate the exact words of a speaker from the rest of the sentence. (Use the colon for quotations of more than one sentence.)

> Taylor said, "I will be able to make worthwhile contributions."
> Ashley asked, "Where are you going?"
> "He is," said the assistant, "going to the office."

Check Your Understanding of Direct Quotations

For each sentence, place commas where needed. If no commas are needed, write C after the sentence.

1. Louisa wrote "We had salad and pizza for dinner."

2. "When" Mariko asked "are you selling your car?"

3. She asked "What are your plans for the future?"

4. Keats wrote "A thing of beauty is a joy forever."

Answers: 1. wrote, **2.** "When,"/asked, **3.** asked, **4.** wrote,

Brevity is Best

The following selection requires three commas and three semicolons. Place them correctly.

Apply It

When you write a business letter you should remember that the person addressed cares only for what we have to say and not for ourselves this is exactly the reverse of a friendly letter. This is why the chief virtue of a business letter is brevity.

Those who read it want to know what we have to say about our business as quickly as possible they want to be able to act on it if it is related in any way to their own business and lose no time.

The Anglo Saxon *bisig* is the word from which are derived both *business* and *busy* a businessperson is supposed to be a busy person. Businesspersons therefore are too busy to read rambling letters where the message is neither clearly stated nor properly formatted.

IMPROVE YOUR VOCABULARY
Prefixes and Roots

Pre means *before* as in *precede*, to go before.

> Precocious, to cook *before*; matured early. (*coquere*, to cook)
> Predict, to tell *before*; foretell. (*dicere*, to tell)
> Preeminent, to project *before*; superior to or surpassing others.
>   (*eminare*, stand out)
> Prelude, to play *before*; a preliminary part. (*ludere*, to play)
> Premonition, to warn *before*; a forewarning. (*monere*, to warn)

Examples

A *precocious* child is literally precooked; that is, his mental faculties are ripened *before* time.

To *predict* is to say in advance or *before* what one believes will happen.

Preeminent means *surpassing* or superior in excellence.

A *prelude* is a playing of a musical introduction *before* the service.

Premonition is literally a "warning *beforehand*."

Other words for recognizing prefixes and roots: precept, precipitate, preclude, predilection, preface, preliminary, preponderance.

Vocabulary Check

Match words with definitions by placing the correct letter in each blank.

_____ 1. precocious   a. to outweigh
_____ 2. predict   b. prematurely developed
_____ 3. preeminent   c. to tell in advance
_____ 4. prelude   d. superior; above all others
_____ 5. premonition   e. a warning
                                       f. an introductory piece of music

16

Punctuation Practice

This lesson is a check-up of the punctuation that you've learned so far.

Commas

Periods

Semicolons

As with the special grammar practice guide, this lesson provides the practice necessary for answering not only correctly but also without hesitation. Be sure to follow these guidelines:

1. Do the exercises orally. <u>Do not mark the sentence itself</u>. The answers are at the end of the lesson, so be sure to check them as needed.

2. Continue to do each practice until you respond not only correctly but without hesitation—until answering correctly becomes a habit.

Exercise

In each sentence, is a comma required at each point indicated by an underscore? Answer YES or NO.

1. There are two possible answers___ and both may be right.
2. We left___ but the others stayed in the pool for a while.
3. He left his money to Jeanne___ and Noah did not receive any.
4. We can go to lunch___ or we can finish our homework.

5. One's participation is important in lobbying Congress___ and the National Committee is a way of making one's voice heard.
6. The rule makes sense___ and yet there are complaints.
7. Jim goes online to shop___ and buys from reputable companies.
8. She has many skills___ but she was not promoted.
9. The city has spent much money on the construction of buildings___ and therefore has a deficit.
10. The newsletter is finished___ and is ready to mail.

Exercise 2

In each sentence, is a semicolon (or period and capital letter) required at each point indicated by an underscore? Answer YES or NO.

1. It is going to snow___ in fact, a blizzard is predicted.
2. It is difficult to read the necessary books on the subject___ still it is not as difficult as it might seem.
3. There are usually two ways of saying something___ both may be right.
4. The test was easy___ that is why everyone passed.
5. At first we were concerned___ then we became worried.
6. They thought it was a computer virus___ still they were not certain.
7. The fax machine___ however, remained in the box.
8. Everyone likes him___ he's always cheerful.
9. We were pleased when you became a member___ however, we noticed that your membership recently lapsed.
10. The head of the department___ nevertheless, still enjoys her work.

Exercise 3

In each sentence, which is required at the underscore—a comma or a semicolon? Answer COMMA or SEMICOLON.

1. Juan always speaks clearly___ no one ever misunderstands him.
2. I plan to leave at 3 p.m.___ consequently, I cannot meet you.
3. We wanted to avoid the heat___ so we drove at night.
4. He has no money___ yet he has talent.
5. Don't complain___ it's not your fault.
6. Give me your hand___ or you'll fall.
7. They were ready to leave the meeting___ but then they changed their minds.
8. The story is untrue___ in fact, it is a lie.
9. This looks bad___ however, you should not give up.
10. The bell rang___ and the light changed.

Exercise 4

In each sentence, is a comma required at each point indicated by an underscore? Answer YES or NO.

1. When it was time to call the meeting___ however, the CEO changed her mind.
2. They had to learn word processing software___ before they could pass the examination.
3. Since the meeting was over___ they decided to stay for some refreshments.
4. When we arrived___ we found that he had resigned.
5. Walking slowly___ I finally reached the top of the hill.
6. As Faith got ready to speak___ she separated her notes.
7. To win the award___ we worked two weeks.
8. When the alarm went off___ the employees ran from the room.
9. When the subordinate clause of a complex sentence comes before the main clause___ separate the two statements by a comma.
10. Do not separate the two statements by a comma___ if the main clause comes first.

Exercise 5

In each sentence, is a comma required at each point indicated by an underscore? Answer YES or NO.

1. The delivery will be made today, tomorrow ___ or Friday.
2. Luke was an honest___ respected lawyer.
3. A check, cash___ or money order will do.
4. They drove an expensive___ bright red sports car.
5. I found a large___ black spider in the drawer.
6. The author was a brilliant___ courageous writer.
7. Aaron was a polite___ helpful employee.
8. The contestant wore a blue___ velvet dress.
9. Mercury, lead___ and tin are metals.
10. It was a cloudy___ threatening day.

Exercise 6

In each sentence, are commas required at the points indicated by the underscores? Answer YES or NO.

1. Mr. Allen___ a board member___ announced the company picnic.
2. My associate___ Thomas Alcott___ is scheduled to arrive at 2 p.m.
3. I must___ however___ disagree with you.
4. This cell phone___ in contrast___ has a color display.

5. They believed___ of course___ that the fire destroyed everything.
6. I must___ therefore___ disagree with you.
7. The four books___ which were lying on the desk___ were dictionaries.
8. The software___ that we are enclosing___ costs $20.
9. Mr. Green___ who speaks Spanish___ is conducting the meeting.
10. The person___ who is computer literate___ can succeed.

Apply It !

Courtesy Counts

Add five commas and one semicolon (or a period and capital letter) to the following letter on courtesy:

It is important that you be courteous since discourtesy injures personal relations. Try to be sincere and direct also do not attempt to get even with a person who has been discourteous to you. Remember that what may sound all right when spoken may be interpreted entirely differently by your reader. For example the following sentence might not have been written discourteously:

We have already explained to you the manner in which your orders are handled by us.

If this sentence however is read aloud in an angry tone the effect is entirely changed. Since discourtesy injures business relations it is important that you be courteous.

IMPROVE YOUR VOCABULARY
Prefixes and Roots

Pro means *for, forth* or *forward*; *pronoun*, for a noun; *provoke*, to call forth; *promote*, to move forward.

Proclaim, *before* plus cry out. (*clamare*, cry out)

Procrastinate, *forward* plus morrow; delay something. (*cras*, tomorrow)

Proficient, to "make *forward*"; highly competent; skilled. (*facere*, to make)

Profuse, to pour *forth*; lavish; dispense liberally. (*fundere*, to pour)

Promulgate, send *forth*; make known; publish. (*mulgere*, to milk)

Examples

To *proclaim* a fact is to call it out *before* everyone.

Procrastinate literally means *forward* plus morrow. To procrastinate therefore means to put off until some future time.

Proficient engineers go *forward* in their professions.

Profuse apologies are poured *forth*.

To *promulgate* is to make known by open declaration, to send *forth*.

Other words for recognizing prefixes and roots: prodigal, profane, profess, progress, prolific, proponent, propose, prosecute, prospect, provide.

Vocabulary Check

Match words with definitions by placing the correct letter in each blank.

_____ 1. proclaim   a. highly qualified; competent

_____ 2. procrastinate   b. to put off to a future time

_____ 3. proficient   c. to announce to everyone

_____ 4. profuse   d. lavish; extravagant

_____ 5. promulgate   e. to make known to everyone

                      f. to support; sustain

The Period, Question Mark, and Exclamation Point

	This lesson covers the period, question mark, and exclamation point.	
17a	**The period for sentence endings, abbreviations, ellipsis marks, and decimal points.**	*Most schools continue to forbid the use of cell phones during class time.*
17b	**The question mark for a direct question, to express doubt, for partly interrogative sentences, and for a series of questions.**	*What caused the accident?*
17c	**The exclamation point after groups of words expressing strong feeling and after interjections.**	*Oh, what a terrible plunge!*

Most likely you know that every sentence should be followed by one of three marks—a period, a question mark, or an exclamation point. But you might not know that a question mark should not follow a polite request. In Lesson 17, you will also find it useful to review such elements as the use of the period for abbreviations, ellipsis marks, and decimal points.

17a The Period for Sentence Endings, Abbreviations, Ellipsis Marks, and Decimal Points

At the end of a declarative sentence or at the end of a command (imperative) sentence, use the period.

> We received your telegram this morning. (Declarative)
> Close the file drawer. (Command)

Periods should be used after the letters in abbreviations. (Omit the periods after the letters in abbreviations such as URL, HTML, DVD, CPU, PIN, and ATM.)

> M.D.   i.e.   R.S.V.P.   e.g.   c.o.d.   et al.   a.m.   U.S.A.

Ellipsis marks show omission in quoted material. Use three spaced periods with one space before and after each period to show an omission in quoted information.

> "The power of attention . . . can be vastly increased."

For the last part of a quoted sentence, use four dots (an ellipsis and a period).

> "Emphasis is placed on the knowledge of computers that is essential. . . . Good teachers are usually aware of this."

Do not use a period in a sentence that already has a period.

> Tess made the presentation at 8 a.m.
> The technician they hired is Clifford Jennings, Jr.

Check Your Understanding of the Period

For each sentence, place periods where needed, and capitalize the beginning of a second sentence. If no period is needed, write C after the sentence.

1. We received your telegram this morning___

2. A fool is a person who is intelligent at the wrong time___

3. She received her Ph___D___ in economics.

4. Read books___ they will do you much good.

5. You should not go___ until the rain stops.

6. Touch this___ it's freezing.

7. You should know why___ we selected this kind of database.

8. Hurry up___ it's getting late.

9. It was unfortunate that Jesse was unable to remember his P___I___N___ when he needed it.

10. The artist will create the design___ you will approve the text.

Answers. 1. period 2. period 3. two periods 4. period/They 5. correct 6. period/It's 7. correct 8. period/It's 9. correct 10. period/You

17b The Question Mark for a Direct Question, to Express Doubt, for Partly Interrogative Sentences, and for a Series of Questions

Use a question mark to indicate the end of a direct question.

> What is the price of these new picture phones?
> Do you think the hurricane will pass through Tampa?

A question mark should not be used for a polite request disguised as a question. A request asks the reader to do a specific action and is answered by having the reader reply to or ignore the request rather than respond with an answer.

> Will you please hold the video conference as soon as possible.
> Will you fill in the enclosed questionnaire and return it by May 30.

The question mark should not be used after an indirect question. To recognize an indirect question, look for such expressions as *ask* or *inquire* used with *if* or *whether*. Notice also that the word order is subject-verb.

> Ramón asked me if I would call his office tomorrow.
> Joyce inquired about the possibility of helping out as a volunteer.
> He asked whether I was interested in his old computer.

The question mark should be used after a question within a statement.

How can we find the folder? was the question on everyone's mind.

The question mark should be used after each separate question in a sentence.

Was the dictionary on the desk? or on the table? or on the shelf?

Check Your Understanding of the Question Mark

For each sentence, place a period or question mark in each blank.

1. I thought she asked whether I was right___

2. I thought she asked, "Are you right___"

3. Have you ever used a handheld computer___

4. "Where did you put the memo ___" was the question I asked the office assistant.

5. Carolyn asked me whether I was fascinated by the theater production ___

6. Will you please walk the dog on your way to school___

7. May I send you a copy of our latest catalog___

8. Please bring me the new messages___

9. Where did you put the incoming correspondence___

10. Did she say, "Tom, I have applied for a new position"___

Answers. 1. period 2. question mark 3. question mark 4. question mark 5. period 6. period 7. period 8. period 9. question mark 10. question mark

17c The Exclamation Point After Groups of Words Expressing Strong Feeling and After Interjections

Place the explanation point after words or groups of words to express strong feeling. Do not, however, overuse it.

Great!
I am so happy to see you!
Congratulations on your new job!

The exclamation point is also placed after interjections. *Oh* is used to express strong feeling and may be followed by either a comma or an exclamation point. The exclamation mark comes at the end of the sentence unless *oh* is to receive emphasis.

Oh, I'm sorry!
Oh! How did you find him?

If the exclamation point is used instead of a period, it is followed by a capital letter. Two spaces should be left after the exclamation point before beginning the next word.

Check Your Understanding of the Exclamation Point

For each sentence, place an exclamation point or a question mark in each blank.

1. Ouch___ Did you see that hornet?

2. Oh, how could he say that___

3. Is there a pencil sharpener somewhere___

4. Hurry___ They just announced our flight.

5. Can anyone tell me where my briefcase is___

6. I was so shocked that I was speechless___

7. Did you ask if there is an ATM machine around here___

8. Will you be able to cash this check___

9. Oh___ What was that awful crash?

10. He is the most despicable character in all literature___

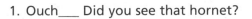

Answers. 1. exclamation point 2. exclamation point 3. question mark 4. exclamation point 5. question mark 6. exclamation point 7. question mark 8. question mark 9. exclamation point 10. exclamation point

Punctuation Pitfalls

In the first section, place a question mark or an exclamation point in each blank space.

In your writing, do you ever leave out a question mark or an exclamation point___ Pity the poor writers who do so habitually___ Are they likely to do well in composition___ Never___ The period is another mark of which we need to say something. No one with a college—or even high school—education should get into the careless habit of putting commas where periods belong.

To make sure that you do not "put commas where periods belong," take this short quiz. In each sentence, cross out any incorrectly used comma, and replace it with a period. Capitalize the first word of the second sentence. Write a C after each correct sentence.

1. Three states gave the railroad its name, it was one of the longest and best systems in the country.

2. We spent several years in Italy, it is called the land of laughter and flowers.

3. Mr. Barlow was born in a small Iowa village, and he is now the president of a large telecommunications company.

4. The house had stood empty for seven years, the former owners had moved to another state.

5. The road is overshadowed by giant trees, they have been growing there for hundreds of years.

6. Despite the severity of the weather, the students came that great distance.

7. We had not driven far when we had a flat tire, this was caused by a nail that we picked up somewhere along the highway.

8. Dr. O'Brien is an instructor at the college, she is also the faculty adviser for the student newspaper.

IMPROVE YOUR VOCABULARY
Prefixes and Roots

Re means again or back: *re*enter, to enter again; *re*call, to call back.

Recognize, to know *again*; to be aware of as known before.
  (*cognoscere*, to know)
Redundant, to surge *back*; to be in excess. (*redundant*, overflow)
Refract, to break *back*; bend back sharply or abruptly.
  (*frangere*, to break)
Reiterate, say *again*; repeat or say repeatedly. (*iterare*, to repeat)
Retail, to cut *again*. (*tailler*, to cut)

Examples

If you *recognize* a person you have seen before, you know him *again*.

If writing is *redundant*, the author has used too many words to express an idea, literally an overflowing or surging *back* or being in excess.

Refraction occurs when a ray of light is deflected, or turned *back*, from its normal path.

Reiterate is to repeat or say over *again*.

A *retailer* is one who sells goods in small parcels or at second hand, literally cutting *again* by small pieces.

Other words for recognizing prefixes and roots: recurrence, respect, retroactive, retrograde, revulsion.

Vocabulary Check

Match words with definitions by placing the correct letter in each blank.

_____ 1. recognize   a. a person who sells goods in small quantities
_____ 2. redundant   b. to repeat again and again
_____ 3. refraction   c. the change from a straight line
_____ 4. reiterate   d. characterized by using too many words
_____ 5. retailer   e. an arbitrator
                 f. remember; to know again

The Apostrophe (Level 1)

This lesson covers the first level of learning the
apostrophe.

| 18a | **The singular possessive.** | *An attorney's fee; anyone's guess* |
| 18b | **The plural possessive.** | *Two attorneys' fees; children's clothing* |

Have you ever worried about where you should place an apostrophe?
You are not alone. The widespread misuse of the apostrophe is generally recognized, one authority estimating that only 10 percent of the
population can place this mark correctly. To know how to use the
apostrophe, study Lesson 18 to learn that you should first decide if
the word is singular or plural before applying one of two rules.

Possessives

Possessives show ownership or possession. "Marie's computer" means
that Marie owns a computer. This is shown by the use of the apostrophe after Marie. To decide if you need to use the apostrophe, reverse
the order of the nouns and place *of* between them.

> Marie's computer = the computer of Marie

The word *possessive*, however, indicates more than ownership. In an
expression such as "a *year's* experience," it is clear that the year did
not possess the experience. Yet the *year* requires an apostrophe. The
apostrophe and *s* may be considered to mean *of a*, *of an*, and *of the*;
in this sense *a year's experience* is regarded as a possessive.

an hour's time   = the time of an hour
a minute's time = the time of a minute
a day's pay   = the pay of a day

The possessive case, however, is not generally used for inanimate objects since they cannot possess anything in the sense that animate objects can. Avoid expressions such as *the apple's stem*, *the lake's shore*, *the table's top*, and *the shop's window*. It is better to use *of the* instead.

the stem of the apple   the shore of the lake

18a The Singular Possessive

If you are writing about a word that means *one thing* and you want to indicate *possession*, add an apostrophe and *s*.

the girl's coat   a fox's tail   a day's work
the firm's policies   last month's prices   next year's plans

Words such as *another*, *anyone*, *someone*, and *everybody* (indefinite pronouns) are always singular and require an apostrophe and *s*.

another's property   anyone's fault   someone's watch

One exception to this rule is found in the following singular nouns in which tradition and the sound of the word govern the use of the apostrophe only:

for appearance' sake
for conscience' sake
for righteousness' sake

Check Your Understanding of the Singular Possessive

In each sentence, circle the correct word from the choices given in parentheses.

1. After an (*hour's*, *hours'*) work, I finished the budget for the department.

2. Forfeiting a (*day's*, *days'*) pay might be too much to ask.

3. He did not get his (*driver's*, *drivers'*) license in time.

4. They were not interested in the other (*person's*, *persons'*) welfare.

5. The newspaper wanted a (*month's*, *months'*) notice for the classified ad.

6. Last (*year's*, *years'*) styles look better on them.

7. We heard (*someone's, someones'*) footsteps behind us.

8. Drill and practice may be part of (*one's, ones'*) training.

9. The (*clown's, clowns'*) antics made the children laugh.

10. Are these peanuts yours or your (*brother's, brothers'*)?

Answers. 1. hour's 2. day's 3. driver's 4. person's 5. month's 6. year's 7. someone's 8. one's 9. clown's 10. brother's

18b The Plural Possessive

If the noun that means *more than one* ends with *s*, add only an apostrophe.

friends' calls	ten minutes' time	two bosses' rules
five days' work	girls' clothing	patients' rights

If the noun that means more than one does not end with *s*, add an apostrophe and *s*.

men's	women's	children's

Check Your Understanding of the Plural Possessive

In each sentence, circle the correct word from the choices given in parentheses.

1. The company paid two (*month's, months'*) salary in advance.

2. The (*womens', women's*) committee is handling the requests.

3. The (*men's, mens'*) organization did not initiate new members.

4. Who has seen the (*children's, childrens'*) skateboards?

5. Several (*manager's, managers'*) notes were locked in the safe.

6. The (*student's, students'*) pictures were published on the front page of the newspaper.

7. Two (*week's, weeks'*) vacation is what the employees received.

8. Most of the (*photographer's, photographers'*) publications were particularly vivid.

Answers. 1. months' 2. women's 3. men's 4. children's 5. managers' 6. students' 7. weeks' 8. photographers'

Apply It !

A proverb is a well-known adage or saying that typically exemplifies a common observation. In each sentence, place an apostrophe correctly for each of the following proverbs.

1. Another persons burden is always light.

2. An idle brain is the devils workshop.

3. Anothers misfortune does not cure my pain.

4. It is a silly goose that comes to a foxs sermon.

5. Industry is fortunes right hand, and frugality her left.

6. Repentance is the hearts medicine.

7. Kind words heal friendships wounds.

8. The noblest task is to command ones self.

9. A prudent haste is wisdoms leisure.

10. Order is heavens first law.

11. Nobodys sweetheart is ugly.

12. A mans home is his castle.

13. The rainbow at night is the shepherds delight.

14. We carry our neighbors failings in sight; we throw our own over our shoulders.

15. One persons loss is another persons gain.

16. At last, the foxes all meet at the furriers.

17. A great mans foolish sayings pass for wise ones.

18. Hope is griefs best music.

19. A kings favor is no inheritance.

20. That which is everybodys business is nobodys business.

IMPROVE YOUR VOCABULARY
Prefixes and Roots

Sub means *under*: *sub*scribe, to write under; *sub*terranean, below the ground. *Sub* also has the forms *suc, suf, sug, sup,* and *sus* as *suc*ceed, *suf*fuse, *sug*gest, *sup*port, *sus*pend.

*Sub*due, take away. (*ducere*, take away)
*Sub*ordinate, to order *under*; below another in rank, importance, and the like. (*ordinare*, to order)
*Sub*poena, *under* penalty; a written legal order for a person to appear in court or be punished. (*poena*, penalty)
*Sub*scribe; to write *under*. (*scribere*, to write)
*Sub*terfuge, to flee *under* or secretly; a plan for hiding or evading. (*fugere*, to flee)

Examples
To *subdue* one's anger is to bring it *under* control.

A *subordinate* is someone *below* another in rank or importance.

To *subscribe* to a magazine is literally to write one's name *under* the order for it.

A *subterfuge* is a scheme for escaping *under* the cover of secrecy; it is any device for evading blame or responsibility.

Other words for recognizing prefixes and roots: submerge, subordinate, subside, subsist, subtract, suburb, suffix, suffocate, supply.

Vocabulary Check

Match words with definitions by placing the correct letter in each blank.

_____ 1. subdue   a. a scheme for evading responsibility
_____ 2. subordinate   b. to write one's name to a paper
_____ 3. subpoena   c. to overcome or conquer
_____ 4. subscribe   d. inferior or below another
_____ 5. subterfuge   e. a document commanding the attendance of a person in court
                       f. prosperity

Lesson ⓵⑨

The Apostrophe (Level 2)

This lesson covers the second level of learning the apostrophe.

19a	Proper nouns.	Lisa's memo is brief.
19b	Joint and separate possession.	Linda and Steve's new boat was just launched. Ethan's and Luisa's applications were sent.
19c	The noun understood.	They met at the doctor's at 3 p.m.
19d	Abbreviations.	The IRS's advice was helpful.

Should you write *Grace's* notes or *Graces'* notes? And should it be the *Smiths'* bill or the *Smith's* bill? This lesson will show you that the rules you will learn in this lesson are the same that you learned in Lesson 18. If the word means one, you would use an apostrophe and *s*, as *Grace's* notes. If the word means more than one, you would use only the apostrophe, as the *Smiths'* bill.

19a Proper Nouns

A **proper noun** distinguishes an individual from others of the same class. Charles, for example, is a proper noun, proper in the sense of "one's own" (it is a person's own name and distinguishes Charles from other people). It is easy to recognize proper nouns since they are always capitalized.

132

For proper **singular** names, follow the rule for singular nouns. If a singular noun ends in *s*, add the *apostrophe* and *s* to the word.

 Marita's computer   *Zoe's notebook*   *William's cell phone*

For proper **plural** names, follow the rule for plural nouns. If a plural noun ends in *s*, add only the apostrophe.

 The Havilands' dog   *The Peets' boat*   *The Burnses' policy*

Some names of places and organizations may omit the apostrophe from possessive nouns:

 Buzzards Bay   *Governors Island*   *The American Bankers Association*

Check Your Understanding of Proper Nouns

In each sentence, circle the correct word from the choices given in parentheses.

1. The police could not find (*Julia's, Julias'*) car.

2. The products can be found at (*Michael's, Michaels'*) store.

3. Ms. (*O'Brien's, O'Briens'*) briefcase was in her office.

4. The (*Rossi's, Rossis'*) lawn was in need of repair.

5. (*Emma's, Emmas'*) office is on the third floor.

6. The sale of Len (*Fox's, Foxs'*) factory was in the local newspaper.

Answers. 1. Julia's **2.** Michael's **3.** O'Brien's **4.** Rossis' **5.** Emma's **6.** Fox's

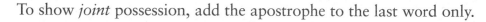

19b Joint and Separate Possession

Add the apostrophe according to whether the possession is joint or separate.

To show *joint* possession, add the apostrophe to the last word only.

 Paul and Fred's father became supervisor.
 We bought it at *Trenwith and Poole's* new store.

To show *separate* possession, add the apostrophe to each noun.

 The bookstore manager set aside *Jacob's and Austin's* books.
 Jessica's and Sophia's compositions received high marks.

Check Your Understanding of Joint and Separate Possession

In each sentence, circle the correct word from the choices given in parentheses.

1. (*Luisa*, *Luisa's*) and Alice's report was on file at the office.

2. The customers bought the items at (*Brown*, *Brown's*) and Taylor's.

3. I met them at my (*aunt*, *aunt's*) and uncle's house.

4. (*Victoria*, *Victoria's*) and Brianna's computers needed repair.

5. The (*producer*, *producer's*) and the director's complaints were justified.

Answers: 1. Luisa 2. Brown 3. aunt 4. Victoria's 5. producer's

19c The Noun Understood

If the second noun is understood, add the apostrophe to the first noun.

> I am going to stay at *Laurie's*. (house)
> Trinity took her daughter to the *dentist's*. (office)

Check Your Understanding of the Noun Understood

In each sentence, circle the correct word from the choices given in parentheses.

1. Ava was at her (*accountant*, *accountant's*).

2. The cousins met at the (*florist's*, *florists*).

3. This tape is (*Stephen's*, *Stephens*).

4. One student's name was William, and the (*other's*, *others*) was Tim.

5. Is going to the (*dentist*, *dentist's*) a terrifying experience?

Answers: 1. accountant's 2. florist's 3. Stephen's 4. other's 5. dentist's

19d Abbreviations

Add an apostrophe and *s* for the singular and an apostrophe for the plural.

Abbreviations follow the same rules for singular and possessive words. You first need to decide whether the abbreviation is singular or plural.

Singular: *NASA's* records are on file.
Plural: All the *CPAs'* requests have been granted.

Check Your Understanding of Apostrophes for Abbreviations

In each sentence, circle the correct word from the choices given in parentheses.

1. At least one (*Ph.D.'s*, *Ph.D.s'*) qualifications were eagerly welcomed.

2. The (*YMCA's*, *YMCAs'*) pool is closed.

3. The (*FDA's*, *FDAs'*) plans were made public.

4. All the (*M.D.'s*, *M.D.s'*) credentials were on file.

5. The (*A.M.A.'s*, *A.M.A.s'*) study of minerals is now available.

Answers: 1. Ph.D.'s 2. YMCA's 3. FDA's 4. M.D.s' 5. A.M.A.'s

A Mark in Distress

Underline any apostrophe errors in the list below. Then write the correct form above each.

Apply It !

   Confusion about the apostrophe can be seen in the striking examples found in signs and correspondence across the country. Someone suggested it would take an army of workers with paintbrushes and a contingent of editors with computers six months to eliminate all the unnecessary apostrophes, reposition the misplaced ones, and insert the necessary ones. Meanwhile, would you help out by fixing these errors:

- Mindy's Sub Shop Open 7 Day's a Week

- Womens and childrens fashion accessories

- A friend of Mr. Kelly

- A CEOs' plan for reorganization

- The Maroney's have gone to Kansas.

- "Ace Funeral Association Takes Care of It's Own." (a slogan)

IMPROVE YOUR VOCABULARY
Prefixes and Roots

Super generally means *beyond*, *above*, or *over* as *super*natural, beyond nature, and *super*vise, to oversee. This prefix often becomes *sur* as in *sur*charge.

> *Super*sede, to sit *over*; to take the place of. (*sedere*, to sit)
> *Super*ficial, *above* the surface. (*facies*, face)
> Supervisor, to see over. (*videre*, see)
> *Sur*plus, *above* more; a quantity over and above what is needed. (*plus*, more)
> *Sur*vive, to live *above*; to remain alive or in existence. (*vivere*, to live)

Examples

The administration appointed new directors to *supersede* or take *over* from the old.

Superficial study touches only the surface or *face* of a matter, not the heart of it.

A *supervisor* looks *over* the work of others.

A *surplus* of anything is that which is *over* and *above* one's needs.

He *survived* his parents, living *over* or *beyond* them.

Other words for recognizing prefixes and roots: supercilious, superfluous, superlative, supervene.

Vocabulary Check

Match words with definitions by placing the correct letter in each blank.

_____ 1. supersede   a. being on the surface
_____ 2. superficial   b. exceeding what is required
_____ 3. supervisor   c. an overseer
_____ 4. surplus   d. one who outlives another
_____ 5. survivor   e. circumstance or condition
                        f. take over or take the place of

The Dash and Parentheses

This lesson covers the dash and parentheses.

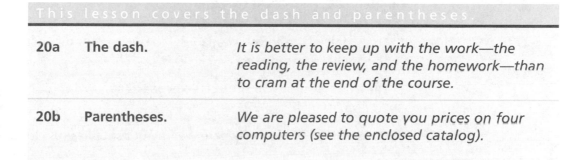

20a	**The dash.**	*It is better to keep up with the work—the reading, the review, and the homework—than to cram at the end of the course.*
20b	**Parentheses.**	*We are pleased to quote you prices on four computers (see the enclosed catalog).*

In this lesson, you will learn important information about dashes and parentheses. A sentence without a dash, for example, may be confusing and unclear as shown in the following example:

Unclear:	These written promises to pay for indeed they are promises are called promissory notes.
Clear:	These written promises to pay—for indeed they are promises—are called promissory notes.

20a The Dash

Use the dash for clarity when explanatory words (appositives) contain commas.

Media events—*news conferences, rallies, and marches*—are sometimes staged for minor reasons.
The three subjects—*management, accounting, and communication*—were scheduled separately.

Use the dash for other reasons—to emphasize certain elements, to indicate an afterthought, or to set off a brief summary.

> He was witty, learned, industrious, and plausible—*everything but honest*. (Emphasis)
> It was obvious that Richard—*in fact, the entire staff*—was in favor of a higher salary schedule. (Afterthought)
> Loyalty, reliability, and diligence—*these are qualities that companies demand of employees*. (Brief summary)

Check Your Understanding of the Dash

For each sentence, write C if correct. If incorrect, replace with the correct punctuation.

1. The whole office force—managers, consultants, and administrative assistants—met at 9 a.m.

2. They take a variety of subjects—keyboarding, law, accounting, and English.

3. Gobbi Office Products—where we buy our supplies—is closed for repairs.

4. Much of what the committee wants to do—supporting local symphonies, improving education, and building churches—is commendable.

5. The report—which consists of fifty pages—is distributed to all employees.

6. They invited us to one meeting—one meeting only—not for the entire convention!

7. I was sure that the receptionist—in fact, all of the office staff—wanted Mark to receive the promotion.

8. Kevin—who works in Goleta—lives in Santa Barbara.

Answers: 1. correct 2. correct 3. Gobbi Office Products, where we buy our supplies, is closed for repairs. 4. correct 5. The report, which consists of fifty pages, is distributed to all employees. 6. correct 7. correct 8. Kevin, who works in Goleta, lives in Santa Barbara.

Note: Use brackets ([ ]) to enclose quoted material added by someone other than the writer, such as comments by the editor. Brackets are used to enclose another's corrections, explanations, or other additional comments.

> "In matters of science he [Jefferson] was more of a dabbler than a philosopher."

20b Parentheses

Use parentheses to give information not related to the main idea of the sentence.

Parentheses are frequently used for references and directions and to set off expressions more completely than commas or dashes.

The pictures of this event (*see Illustration 8*) are enclosed.
She wrote about the incident in her article (*page 6*).

Use parentheses to enclose enumerated items that precede items in a series.

They planned to study (*1*) *the period,* (*2*) *the comma, and* (*3*) *the semicolon.*

When the parenthetical matter is a sentence within a sentence, follow these rules:

1. Do not capitalize the first word unless it is a proper noun.

   I would like you to study Mr. Gray's letter (a copy of it is enclosed) in which he states he cannot return the computers.

2. Do not use a period at the end of the parenthetical sentence, although you may include a question mark or an exclamation point.

   You can find the information in the brochure (pages 15 through 26).

Check Your Understanding of Parentheses

For each sentence, write C if correct. If incorrect, replace with the correct punctuation.

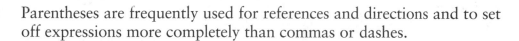

1. Thomas Adams (1818–1905) is the inventor of chewing gum.

2. The punctuation *after* a parenthesis (see the last sentence) must be the same as it would be if there were no parenthesis.

3. The author stated, "Advancement opportunities are shrinking along with corporate payrolls" (Jones, 1989, p. 211) but offered no suggestions.

4. Three of the most effective workers (Lauren Solomon, Manuel Patel, and Glenn Hills) left the company.

5. July payrolls showed a sharp split (see chart).

6. A noun (page 38) is the name of a person, place, or thing.

7. They take a variety of subjects (law, keyboarding, and Spanish).

8. All the arrangements (the time, the location, and the menu) have been settled.

Apply It !

Abused Marks of Punctuation

Insert parentheses and dashes where they should be placed. Add two single dashes, two sets of dashes, and one set of parentheses.

Now we have to consider the dash a much-abused mark of punctuation. Our thoughts may be running on smoothly when we suddenly digress and unbelievable as it may seem need a mark to indicate the abruptness of the change. You see how our sentences become examples of their own rules concerning other marks of punctuation. Merely remarking that the dash is used generally in enumerations, we will also discuss other instances where there may be doubt as to the best usage dashes in pairs and parentheses.

When we come to discuss parentheses see page 81 for a fuller discussion of this subject, we find that it is sometimes convenient to break into a sentence with an "aside" grammatically independent of the main statement. But sometimes and this sentence is a case in point two dashes are preferable, for they indicate a close connection between the "aside" and the sentence it interrupts.

IMPROVE YOUR VOCABULARY
Prefixes and Roots

Trans means *over* or *beyond*: *transfer*, to carry over; *transatlantic*, beyond the Atlantic.

Transgress, to step *over*; to violate a law. (*gradi*, to step)

Transient, to go *beyond*; temporary. (*ire*, to go)

Transcend, climb *over*; to go beyond the limits; exceed.
   (*scandere*, to climb)

Translucent, to shine through. (*lucere*, to shine)

Transpose, place *over*; to change the usual order or position of.
   (*pos*, place)

Examples

A *transgression* is a stepping *over* the limits of civilized behavior.

Transient tenants are those who are going on *through* or *beyond* a place.

If athletes *transcend* their records of the previous year, they climb above or *over* it.

Glass is *translucent* because light can shine *through* it.

To *transpose* two objects is to put or place each *over* in the other's position.

Other words for recognizing prefixes and roots: transcribe, transparent, transfusion, transit, transmute, transplant.

Vocabulary Check

Match words with definitions by placing the correct letter in each blank.

_____ 1. transgress   a. to offend by violation of a rule
_____ 2. transient   b. to change the place or order of
_____ 3. transcend   c. permitting light to shine through
_____ 4. translucent   d. non-permanent boarder
_____ 5. transpose   e. a fresh-water fish
                       f. to rise above a previous record; surpass

The Colon

This chapter covers two main reasons to punctuate with the colon.

The colon for statements or lists.

The colon is usually a mark of formality, its main uses being statements or lists, quotations of more than one sentence, and the salutation of a business letter. In Lesson 21, you will learn that the colon used before any group of words means *here follows an example or illustration*.

The Colon for Statements or Lists

Use the colon after such expressions as *in the following manner* or any introduction that means *as follows*.

> The three basic principles of accounting are as follows: materiality, objectivity, and relevance.
> This is what I wanted to know: when are we going to have the debate?

Capitalize the first letter of each item in a list when the list is in column form.

> You should be familiar with the following computer terms:
>
> • Software   • Cookie
> • Compatibility   • Firewall

Use lowercase letters when the items are not in column form.

> You should be familiar with the following computer terms: software, compatibility, cookie, and firewall.

Do not use the colon after *is*, *are*, or *were* or before series that are not explanatory words (appositives):

> The first three days of the week are Sunday, Monday, and Tuesday.
> He knows such languages as Spanish, Italian, and Russian.

The use of the colon in separating the clauses of a sentence has been largely replaced by a semicolon or treated as a separate sentence. An example follows:

> *Original*:   The weather was far from favorable: thunderstorms were rising in the east.
> *Modern use*:   The weather was far from favorable; thunderstorms were rising in the east.

If the statement is a formal rule or principle, a quotation, or consists of more than one statement, it should begin with a capital letter. Otherwise, it may begin with a lowercase letter.

> Here is a key rule: When no difficulty results, use *that* with a necessary clause and *which* with an unnecessary clause.

Note: Use the colon after the salutation in a business letter with mixed punctuation. Mixed punctuation adds a colon after the salutation and a comma after the complimentary closing.

> Dear Mr. Wilson:

Check Your Understanding of Colons

For each sentence, write C if correct. If incorrect, write the sentence correctly.

1. People can avoid these simple mistakes: the arithmetic error, the spelling error, and the capitalization error.

2. Several questions should be asked before deciding on a program: Is it feasible? Is it effective?

3. The section now reads as follows: "Employees should be punctual for the weekly meetings."

4. Still abundant were: fruit, vegetables, and herbs.

5. They must please the following interest groups: subscribers, advertisers, and owners.

6. They searched for such items as: pens, pencils, and rulers.

7. The map gave these directions: Turn left at the underpass; then go five miles until the lights.

8. The last and most important rule is this: When in doubt, consult the dictionary.

Answers. 1. correct 2. correct 3. correct 4. Still abundant were fruit, vegetables, and herbs. 5. correct 6. They searched for such items as pens, pencils, and rulers. 7. correct 8. correct

Apply It !

Clarifying Colons

Insert colons where they should be placed. A total of six is needed.

The colon has two uses It is used before a formal quotation or enumeration. It is infrequently used between two clauses of a sentence in which the second stands in some sort of apposition with the first. We need not go far for an illustration of the second use the very sentence we write furnishes it.

To make sure you are not confused by the colon, insert a colon where needed in each of the following sentences. If not needed, write a C.

1. Among the qualities everyone should develop are these tact, loyalty, perseverance, and resourcefulness.

2. This is our advice Stay in school and prepare for a career.

3. The seasons of the year are fall, winter, spring, and summer.

4. These are the four courses you should take English, algebra, chemistry, and accounting.

5. The five Great Lakes are Lake Erie, Lake Ontario, Lake Huron, Lake Michigan, and Lake Superior.

6. Wanted experienced accountant.

IMPROVE YOUR VOCABULARY
Roots and Prefixes

As you have learned, a **prefix** is something added to the beginning of some other word. A **root,** however, is the main part of the word. For the following sections, study each root and its sample word (for example **CAP, CEP, CIP: take; seize; grasp**), and note the prefixes listed. Both the root and the prefixes should give you enough clues to determine the meaning of each word.

CAP, CEP, CIP: take; seize; grasp

Prefixes

> *ante* (*anti*): before
> *ex*: out
> *in* (*im*): in, not
> *re*: again, back

Examples

"Do not *anticipate* trouble" means "Do not expect (*take*) trouble before it comes."

A *capable* employee can *take* hold of any appropriate job.

An *exception* is something *taken* out of the usual run of events.

An *imperceptible* sound is one that the ear cannot catch or *seize*.

An *incipient* cold is one that is just beginning to *take* hold.

Vocabulary Check

For each sentence, fill each blank with an appropriate word from the list at the right.

1. A _____ is essentially a container.
2. If you have a _____ mind, you will easily grasp the idea of the passage.
3. If you are _____ to illnesses, you catch infections easily.
4. A _____ is a set of instructions about required ingredients. "*Take* one pint of cream and a quart of strawberries . . ."
5. A football player _____ a pass when he catches it in the air between two of his opponents.

intercepts
receptacle
receptive
recipe
susceptible

The Hyphen

This chapter covers punctuating with the hyphen.		
22a	**Compound words.**	<u>No-fault</u> insurance was not offered.
22b	**Compound numbers from 21 to 99.**	There were <u>thirty-five</u> items on the test.
22c	**Unit measures.**	It was a <u>50-mile</u> journey.
22d	**The prefixes *self*, *ex*, and *all*.**	The subject of <u>self-esteem</u> was not included in the discussion.

Someone once said, "To use the hyphen incorrectly or to omit it when it should be used is not an error of which to be ashamed." Yet the question comes up frequently, and in Lesson 22 you will find out what you should do.

22a Compound Words

Use hyphens with "permanently" hyphenated words, such as "long-term." Use hyphens with "temporary" words not shown in the dictionary but used together as an adjective before a noun.

Permanent Compounds. Some permanently hyphenated words, such as "long-term," require the use of the dictionary to verify their correctness. With these words, always use hyphens—whether they appear before or after the nouns or pronouns they modify. The *long-term* goals of the students were discussed. Their clothing was always *up-to-date*.

Here are several more permanent compounds:

part-time	*part-time work*
small-scale	*small-scale operation*
no-fault	*no-fault insurance*
hands-off	*hands-off policy*

Temporary Compounds. Other words are not shown in the dictionary but are used together as an adjective before a noun—most often for clarity. The phrase *slow moving traffic*, for example, is unclear. Does it mean traffic with the characteristics of slowness or that traffic now is moving slowly? If it means the latter, *slow-moving traffic* should be used so that the reader need not hesitate in reading.

Here are other examples of temporary compounds that contribute to clarity:

two-bedroom house	*fund-raising appeals*	*clean-water bill*

In addition, compounds with *well-*, *ill-*, *better-*, *best-*, *little-*, *lesser-*, and the like are hyphenated before the noun unless the expression has a modifier, such as *a* very *well known person*.

well-known person	*little-known facts*	*lower-credit quality*
ill-advised trip	*best-performing stocks*	*higher-quality goods*
better-known writings	*worst-performing stocks*	*well-established practice*

Omit the hyphen if the words follow the noun or if the first word ends in *ly*.

> The system of seniority is company wide.
> We saw the slowly rising sun.
> They are well known.
> The trip was ill advised.

Check Your Understanding of Compound Words

In each sentence, insert hyphens where they should be placed. If no hyphen is needed, write C after the sentence.

1. The salesperson went from *house to house*.

2. The report had been *well researched*.

3. The *highly developed* program became lost.

4. They paid taxes the *old fashioned* paper way.

5. The *so called* agreements have been delayed.

6. The policy relies on a system that is *well established*.

7. Jim is an *accident prone* person.

8. The *higher quality* goods sold quickly.

Answers. 1. correct 2. correct 3. correct 4. old-fashioned 5. so-called 6. correct 7. accident-prone 8. higher-quality

22b Compound Numbers from 21 to 99

Use the hyphen in compound numbers from 21 to 99 when they are in word form.

> twenty-two invoices   thirty-five years old   sixty-nine checks

Check Your Understanding of Compound Numbers From 21 to 99

In each sentence, insert hyphens where they should be placed. If no hyphen is needed, write C after the sentence.

1. The tape cost only *forty nine* cents.

2. The accountant plans to retire when she is *sixty six*.

3. The sisters spent only *thirty five* dollars for the gift.

4. Among the supplies missing were *ninety four* staplers.

Answers. 1. forty-nine 2. sixty-six 3. thirty-five 4. ninety-four

22c Unit Measures

Use a hyphen in compound adjectives formed by joining a number (written out or expressed in figures) to a word indicating a unit measure.

> Our two-year lease will soon expire.
> Several drivers exceeded the 30-mile-an-hour speed limit.

Check Your Understanding of Unit Measures

In each sentence, insert hyphens where they should be placed. If no hyphen is needed, write C after the sentence.

1. The *five month long* strike was suddenly over.

2. It was the biggest *three month* gain in two years.

3. A *ten minute* conversation followed.

4. The *twelve day* trip will begin September 12.

5. Raul's fastball was clocked as a *90 mile an hour* pitch.

6. We were fortunate to get a *15 year* mortgage.

Answers. 1. five-month-long 2. three-month 3. ten-minute 4. twelve-day 5. 90-mile-an-hour 6. 15-year

22d The Prefixes *Self, Ex,* and *All*

Use the hyphen between *self*, *ex*, and *all* and between a prefix and a proper noun, such as pro-French.

> self-discipline   all-powerful   pre-Renaissance
> ex-chairperson   self-help   un-American

Check Your Understanding of the Prefixes *Self, Ex,* and *All*

In each sentence, insert hyphens where they should be placed. If no hyphen is needed, write C after the sentence.

1. The measures were found to be *self defeating*.

2. Attention focused on the *ex president*.

3. The writing was considered *un American*.

4. They considered themselves *all powerful*.

Answers. 1. self-defeating 2. ex-president 3. un-American 4. all-powerful

Apply It !

Insert hyphens where they should be placed. Three hyphens are required.

In addition to contributing to clarity, the use of the hyphen can also contribute to conciseness and emphasis, a little known fact. Study the sentence that follows:

The teachers have gone to a meeting that will last for three hours.

Now if you wish to emphasize *teachers* and *three hours*, this sentence is fine. But if you wish to emphasize *teachers* and *meeting*, you should spotlight the word *meeting* at the end of the sentence—and using the long lived hyphen can make this possible. It can also result in conciseness, a savings of four words.

The teachers have gone to a three hour meeting.

IMPROVE YOUR VOCABULARY
Roots With Prefixes

CEDE, CEED, CESS: move, go, yield

Prefixes

ac (*ad*): to, at, toward
ante: before
con: with, together
ex: out, out of, from
pre: before
inter: among, between
se: away from

Examples

An antecedent is the word that *goes* before a pronoun and thus identifies it.

To *concede* is to admit or *yield* that another person may be right.

To *intercede* in a quarrel is to *move* in between the two disputants, with the idea of settling the dispute.

Precede means to *go* before someone.

After the flood, the water quickly receded or *moved* back.

Vocabulary Check

For each sentence, fill each blank with an appropriate word from the list at the right.

1. To _____ to another's wishes requires some yielding.
2. To _____ down the street in a procession is simply to move forward.
3. When motorists _____ the speed limit, they go beyond it.
4. If you have _____ to a friend's swimming pool, you may go into it at will.
5. To _____ is to move away or withdraw from a group or association.

accede
access
exceed
proceed
secede

Quotation Marks and Italics

This lesson covers punctuation with question marks and italics.

23a	**Quotation marks for direct quotations.**	*The author explained, "I prefer to write mysteries."*
23b	**Quotation marks for articles, chapters, short stories, and the like.**	*The class read the article entitled "Fitness."*
23c	**Italics for books, magazines, and newspapers.**	*I always read <u>The Wall Street Journal</u>.*

It is sometimes difficult to know whether to use quotation marks or italics. In Lesson 23, however, you will learn that quotation marks are used for direct quotations and for subdivisions of larger units. In contrast, italics are used for larger units such as books, magazines, and newspapers.

23a Quotation Marks for Direct Quotations

Use quotation marks to enclose the exact words of a person.

> "Fidelity is seven-tenths of business success," James Parton held.
> Shakespeare said, "To thine own self be true."
> Shakespeare said that we should be true to ourselves.

Notice that only the exact words of a person are enclosed in quotation marks.

Place periods and commas *inside* quotation marks. Place all other punctuation *outside* unless it is part of the original quotation.

> Tyler said, "I will go." [period inside quotation marks]
> "I will go," he said. [comma inside quotation marks]
> Did she ask, "Where are you going"? [question mark outside quotation marks]
> They spoke of the "eerie light"; I became alarmed. [semicolon outside quotation marks]

Use single quotations to set off a quotation within a quotation.

> "I think," he said, "that it was Pope who said 'To err is human.'"

Check Your Understanding of Quotation Marks for Direct Quotations

For each sentence, write C if correct. If incorrect, make the necessary corrections.

1. My mother said that I should have known better.

2. "Let us hope," we said, "that the vote is favorable."

3. Mr. Gibson replied that he would need students for summer work.

4. Have you ever written a report? the instructor asked.

5. The lawyer's plea was that we should avoid litigation.

6. "Lefthanders have always had to struggle in a society designed for right-handers," the author claimed.

7. The speaker said that the great remedy for anger is delay.

8. Demas said, Nothing succeeds like success.

Answers. 1. correct. 2. correct 3. correct. 4. "Have you ever written a report?" 5. correct 6. correct 7. correct 8. "Nothing succeeds like success."

23b Quotation Marks for Articles, Chapters, Short Stories,

Use quotation marks with the names of articles, chapters, short stories, short poems, and the like. Think of them as subdivisions of whole publications such as books, newspapers, and magazines, which require italics.

> Please send me "Mutual Funds," a recent article.
> Students read "Eating Wisely," a chapter in their new book.
> I just finished reading "The Pit and the Pendulum," a short story.
> Ellen just mailed me "15 Houseplants Even You Can't Kill," a small pamphlet.

Check Your Understanding of Quotation Marks for Articles, Chapters, Short Stories, and the Like

For each sentence, write C if correct. If incorrect, make the necessary corrections.

1. Not on the list was "Advertising Success," a chapter in the text.

2. The article "Executive Pay" was included.

3. Have you read *To Build a Fire*, a short story by Jack London?

4. My instructor recommended the article *Workplace Ergonomics*.

5. Students are required to buy *The Wall Street Journal*, a popular business publication.

6. Included on the list was *Depreciation*, a chapter in the text.

7. Last week's featured article, "Pensions," was informative.

8. The subscribers had read the editorial *The Flu Shot Shortage*.

Answers. 1. correct. 2. correct 3. "To Build a Fire." 4. "Workplace Ergonomics." 5. correct 6. "Depreciation," 7. correct 8. "The Flu Shot Shortage."

23c Italics for Books, Magazines, and Newspapers

Italicize (or underline if italics are not available) the titles of books, magazines, newspapers, and other complete published or artistic works.

I sometimes read *The Washington Post*.
I sometimes read <u>The Washington Post</u>.

Check Your Understanding of Italics for Books, Magazines, and Newspapers

In each sentence, write C if correct. If incorrect, make the necessary corrections. Use an underline to indicate italics.

1. She often read *Scientific American*, a popular magazine.

2. My brother has not received a bill for *The Cincinnati Inquirer*.

3. *Health Matters*, a new magazine, featured the article "Sports Nutrition."

4. Students enjoyed reading "Thereby Hangs a Tale," an informative book about word origins.

5. Did you see the editorial in *The Tampa Tribune*?

6. We sometimes buy *Newsweek*, a popular news magazine.

7. Stevenson's famous *Treasure Island* was on the booklist.

8. The group was reading "One Hundred Ways to Cut Expenses," a timely book.

9. Two magazines on the recommended list are *Computing* and *Naturelink*.

10. The class read the popular book "The Great Gatsby."

Answers. 1. correct 2. correct 3. correct 4. Thereby Hangs a Tale 5. correct 6. correct 7. correct 8. One Hundred Ways to Cut Expenses 9. correct 10. The Great Gatsby

Note: Use quotation marks or italics for short expressions. When short expressions such as "a vicious circle" need to be emphasized, use quotation marks or italics or underlining.

The word "nice" has a curious history.
The word *nice* has a curious history.
The word <u>nice</u> has a curious history.

Apply It !

Add the necessary quotation marks and italics (use an underline to indicate italics) to the following sales message.

Physicians, nurses, and health care professionals—all make a claim for one of the best nutritional magazines on the market today—Nutrition Today. Dr. Jonathon Lopez states, I am a regular reader of this magazine and can honestly say it has no equal.

Nutrition Today can be described as an educational magazine, providing readers with practical information about diet, lifestyle, vitamins, minerals, and other nutrients. Recently, it has published outstanding articles such as Nutrient Profile and Science Update. In the past year, it has also featured such articles as Sports Nutrition: Stocking Your Sports Medicine Chest, The New Vitamin on the Block, and Treatment Plan for the Cold.

Be sure therefore to order Nutrition Today. It is a decision you will never regret. As Dr. Lopez maintains, It has no equal.

IMPROVE YOUR VOCABULARY
Common Roots with Prefixes

DICT: speak, say

Prefixes

in: in
contra: against
e, ex: out
pre: before

Examples

Diction is the manner of expression in words, a way of *saying* things.

The *predicate* of a sentence is that part that makes a *statement* about the subject; the subject comes before it.

When a jury gives a *verdict*, it brings in a true "*saying*" or opinion of a case.

An *edict* is a proclamation, a "*saying* out."

To *contradict* is to *speak* against something.

Vocabulary Check

For each sentence, fill each blank with an appropriate word from the list at the right.

1. A _____ is one who dictates, especially a ruler or tyrant with absolute power.
2. To _____ is to say in advance what one believes will happen.
3. A _____ is the student who delivers the valedictory speech at graduation.
4. To _____ something is to direct attention to or point out.
5. To _____ is to speak something aloud for someone else to write down.

dictate
dictator
indicate
predict
valedictorian

Capitalization

24a	Capitalize the first word of every sentence.	*Honesty is the best policy.*
24b	Capitalize proper nouns.	*There are many American colleges.*

It is sometimes difficult to know whether to capitalize a word or not. You should usually capitalize the first words in sentences and always capitalize proper nouns. The names of the months are capitalized, but the seasons of the year are not. Study Lesson 24 to learn more about this important subject.

24a

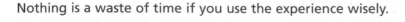

Nothing is a waste of time if you use the experience wisely.

Also capitalize the first word of a line of poetry.

True ease in writing comes from art, not chance,
As those move easiest who have learned to dance.

—Pope, *Essay on Criticism, II*

Capitalize the first word of a quoted sentence. When the quotation is interrupted by an expression such as "he said," do not capitalize what follows as "a nice day . . ." in the second sentence.

The official said, "There is a great deal in the first impression."
"It is," he said, "a nice day for reading."

Check Your Understanding of the First Word of a Sentence

For each sentence, write C if correct. If incorrect, make the necessary corrections.

1. "Coherence," the author said, "is attained in three ways."

2. When you reach Buffalo (It will probably be 9 p.m.), be sure to call.

3. The author wrote, "Working at home has become epidemic."

4. "The reality is less romantic," he said, "But that has not stopped millions of Americans from it."

5. It was many and many a year ago
In a kingdom by the sea . . .

Answers. 1. correct 2. (it will probably be 9 p.m.) 3. correct 4. but 5. correct

Note: Capitalize the first word of the salutation and complimentary close of a letter.

Dear Mr. Hammond: Sincerely,

24b Capitalize Proper Nouns

An important rule is that proper nouns begin with capitals and common nouns with small letters. You can see the difference in the following examples:

David took the CPA exam.
The accountant took the CPA exam.

David is a person's own name, the name that belongs to him and by which he is distinguished from other people. It is therefore called a **proper noun**—proper in the sense of "one's own."

Accountant, on the other hand, is not the name of a particular person. It is a general name for any one of a class of people and is therefore called a **common noun.**

Proper nouns include the following:

Dates and events such as days of the week, months of the year, historical events, and holidays.

February	Wednesday	The Civil War
The Fourth of July	August	Monday, July 24

Geographical locations such as cities, states, countries, streets, lakes, rivers, oceans, and mountains.

Denver	Phillips Avenue	Pacific Ocean
Colorado	Lake Erie	Rocky Mountains
United States	Nile River	the East

Organizations such as business, civic, educational, and governmental agencies, and the like.

Congress	House of Representatives
Senate	Supreme Court
Harvard University	Center for the Performing Arts
Microsoft Corp.	Internet

Titles when they precede and are used directly with a person's name. To show respect, however, the titles of high government and church officials may be capitalized. But do not capitalize titles when they do not precede and are not used directly with a person's name.

I met Doctor Grayson and another doctor whose name I have forgotten.
The Speaker of the House uses great power.
I worked as a kindergarten teacher last spring.

Words naming **family relationships** when they are followed by the name. When the word naming family relationships is preceded by *the*, *a*, *an* or by such words as *my* or *their*, do not capitalize.

In the past, Aunt Ellie talked with Grandmother Taylor every day.
My aunt Sally did not call often.

Academic subjects when they are specific courses or when they contain a proper noun. But do not capitalize such subjects when they are used to denote studies in general or common divisions of knowledge.

They studied English, French, and Freshman Mathematics I.
They studied accounting, management, and computer applications.

Literary or artistic works such as books, plays, and magazines. Capitalize every word except coordinating conjunctions, articles, and short prepositions. Capitalize the initial article if it is part of the official name.

> How to Buy Stocks
> The Copy Center of the Future

The title of complete works may be printed in all capital letters as an alternative to italics or underlining.

> ENGLISH GRAMMAR has many valuable guidelines.

Capitalize **North, East, South,** and **West** when they refer to specific regions in the United States. But do not capitalize nouns or adjectives simply indicating direction.

Capitalize	Do Not Capitalize
the South	the southern part of Maine
the North	traveling north of the highway
the East	The sun rises in the east.
the West	western Minnesota
the Northeast	the northern part of California

Check Your Understanding of Proper Nouns and Adjectives

For each sentence, underscore words needing capitalization. For correct sentences, write C after the sentence.

1. If they travel far enough north, they will reach Montpelier.

2. The president of Loon Mountain Company appointed a new assistant.

3. The Federal Bureau of Investigation was named in the suit.

4. Gloria was born in the Southeastern part of Texas.

5. He answered Dean Russell's letter promptly.

6. We studied history, mathematics, and English.

7. She met Dr. Annette Howe, a Professor at the college.

8. The assistant manager had called the company.

9. The largest college in New York City is Columbia University.

10. The vice president of the company lives in the east.

Note: Do not capitalize the second half of a compound sentence following a semicolon.

Talent is something; tact is everything.
Using the most efficient method is like swimming with the current; you progress faster while expending less effort.

Note: Do not capitalize the names of the seasons.

fall, spring, winter, summer

Apply It !

Place eighteen additional capital letters in the following letter.

Ms. Erin Rains
39 Locust Street
Boysford, ID 03702-0313

Dear Ms. Rains:

As you are one of our preferred customers, we are telling you about courtesy days, the august furniture sale that will begin thursday, august 7. We would like our charge customers to have first choice of the great values before they are announced to the public.

We hope therefore that you will join us on one of our three courtesy days—thursday, friday, and saturday of this week—when you may come in and make your selections at the sale prices.

You will find greater variety than usual because we now carry popular brands such as timberline and natura world. You will also find attractive prices this year. We look forward to having you visit us on the most important event of our year—courtesy days!

sincerely,

IMPROVE YOUR VOCABULARY
Common Roots with Prefixes

DUCT, DUC: lead, bring, draw

Prefixes

ab: away
con: together
de: down from
e: out
in: in, on, into
pro: forward
re: back again
se: away

Examples

If someone tries to *induce* you to gamble, do not be *led* astray.

A *duct*ile substance can be *drawn* or led without breaking.

To *conduct* is to *lead* together or the act of guiding or leading.

To *educate* is to *lead* out, for example, to bring forth the best capabilities of the student.

The tear *ducts bring* tears from the tear glands to the eyes.

Vocabulary Check

For each sentence, fill each blank with an appropriate word from the list at the right.

1. To _____ is to lead away; to kidnap.
2. A _____ is something produced by nature or made by art.
3. To _____ is to lead down; to take away or subtract.
4. To _____ is to lead apart; to tempt to wrongdoing.
5. To _____ is to lead back; to lessen as in size or price.

abduct
deduct
product
reduce
seduce

Lesson 25

Numbers

This lesson covers punctuation for numbers.

25a	**Certain numbers written out.**	*Twenty-seven students received library cards.*
25b	**Figures for certain numbers.**	*The company lost 20 percent of its business.*
25c	**Dates.**	*February 6 was her birthday.*

The correct use of numbers depends on the kind of material in which they appear. Numbers are used sparingly in literature and ordinary text matter but more frequently in business, technical, and scientific writing. Study Lesson 25 to discover what you should do.

25a Certain Numbers Written Out
Write out:

- A number that begins a sentence.

  Fourteen questions were on the examination.

- Simple fractions.

  They could fill only *one third* of the order.

- Approximations that can be expressed in one or two words.

  They had won over a *million* dollars.

164

- Ages of persons.

  She was *thirty-five* years old.

- Numbers from one to ten for business and technical writing.

  The workers received benefits for *six* weeks.

- Numbers from one to ninety-nine for ordinary text.

  The temperature rose *fifteen* degrees in less than an hour.

25b Figures for Certain Numbers

Use figures for:

- Numbers of volumes and pages.

  See *Volume II, page 226*.

- Dates, street numbers, and the like.

  It happened on *April 13, 2002*.

- Fractions used with whole numbers.

  They ordered *2½* yards of material.

- Percentages and decimals.

  9 percent discount   *12.500* of the total

- Ages of persons if the age appears after a person's name or if it is used in a technical sense.

  Lee Steadman, *40*, was involved in an accident.

- When several numbers appear in a sentence, the rule for the larger number should apply to all numbers.

  Of the *30* employees who attended, *20* were working as specialists, *7* were classified as assistants, and *3* were employed as executives.

- Numbers over ten for business and technical writing.

  There are *12* months in a year.

- Numbers over ninety-nine for ordinary text.

The report contained *110* pages.

Check Your Understanding of Certain Numbers Written Out and Figures for Certain Numbers

For each sentence, circle the correct number in the enclosed parentheses.

1. (*31*, *Thirty-one*) students were awarded special honors.
2. Harry McGee, a sophomore, is only (*19*, *nineteen*) years old.
3. She received only (*4*, *four*) percent discount on her account.
4. He found the quotation on page (*6*, *six*).
5. The company received (*3½*, *three and a half*) boxes of the new software.
6. Rents for the office have risen (*35*, *thirty-five*) percent.
7. She needs (*50*, *fifty*) cents from the register.
8. They found that (*¼*, *one fourth*) of the order was defective.
9. Jim ordered 12 sheets of paper, 24 envelopes, and (*3*, *three*) stamps.
10. Only (*7*, *seven*) people are in the room.

Answers: 1. Thirty-one 2. nineteen 3. 4 percent 4. page 6 5. 3½ boxes 6. 35 percent 7. 50 cents 8. one fourth 9. 3 stamps 10. 7 people

Note: Write out amounts $1 and over in figures as $1,500.95. Write amounts of money less than $1 in figures combined with the word cents as 20 cents.

I spent 75 cents for a glue stick.
The price of the color printer was $350.

Note: Do not add a decimal and two zeroes to whole dollar amounts:

We donated $230 to the disaster relief fund.
The store charged $5 to rent the video.

25c Dates

Use cardinal figures (1, 2, 3, and the like) when the day is written after the month.

A common error is to use 1st, 2nd, or 3rd, and the like when the day is written after the month.

Incorrect: January 25th, 2005
Correct: January 25, 2005

Do not be misled by the pronunciation of the number.

Use ordinal figures (1st, 2nd, 3rd, and the like) if the day appears before the month or alone.

We expected to hear from you before the 4th of June.

Check Your Understanding of Dates

For each sentence, circle the correct number in the enclosed parentheses.

1. The next meeting will be held on February (*6, 6th*).
2. Your order will be shipped to you by the (*15, 15th*) of this month.
3. We hope to hear from you by the (*21, 21st*) of September.
4. The payment is due on April (*6, 6th*).
5. November (*21, 21st*), 1985, is the date of her birth.
6. Your June (*16, 16th*) payment is late.
7. My sister intended to book the flight before the (*11, 11th*) of July.
8. Our plans include an anniversary party on June (*28, 28th*).

Answers. 1. February 6. 2. 15th 3. 21st 4. April 6. 5. November 21 6. June 16 7. 11th 8. June 28

Name That Number

Cross out any incorrectly written number, and write in the correct one in this portion of a business letter. Find five errors.

Apply It

     Dr. Francis asked that we send her 65 copies of our latest brochure. She

is conducting 4 workshops and believes that over ten teachers will attend

each workshop.

     The cost of the brochures is $225.00. There is a ten percent discount if the

bill is paid before April 30th. It is disappointing that only ½ the class plans to

attend. We will be happy to send Dr. Francis the 65 copies.

IMPROVE YOUR VOCABULARY
Roots and Prefixes

FAC, FACT, FECT, FIC: do, make

Prefixes

> *ad* (af): to
> *con*: with, together
> *de*: down
> *dif*: not
> *e, ex* (ef): out
> *per*: through, by

Examples

> If one is *affected* by sadness, one's feelings have had something *done* to them.

> A *confectioner* is someone who puts together something, such as *making* candy or other confections.

> An *efficient* person "gets things *done*," producing outward effects.

> A *facsimile* of a document is *made* as similar as possible to the original.

> To *manufacture* is literally to *make* by hand.

> *Fiction* is *make*-believe.

Vocabulary Check

For each sentence, fill each blank with an appropriate word from the list at the right.

1. An _____ person gets thing done, producing outward effects.
2. That which is _____ is done thoroughly and well.
3. To _____ one's job by acquiring better tools is to make the job easier to do.
4. _____ means *not* easy to do.
5. When you say that a little money will _____ for a trip, you mean that "it will do."

difficult
efficient
facilitate
perfect
suffice

You cannot hope to succeed as an amanuensis or hold a position of any importance unless you are qualified to spell, punctuate, and capitalize correctly and write the English language with a reasonable degree of accuracy.

—G. S. Kimball, *Kimball's Business English*

Spelling

Do You Make These Mistakes in Spelling?

WRONG	RIGHT
It's *to* good *too* be true.	It's *too* good *to* be true.
Their writing on your paper.	*They're* writing on your paper.
The desks were *stationery*.	The desks were *stationary*.
The decision *effected* many.	The decision *affected* many.
The *principle* of the school spoke.	The *principal* of the school spoke.
Do not *loose* it.	Do not *lose* it.
It's appearance was a surprise.	*Its* appearance was a surprise.

It hardly seems necessary to say that spelling is important. It is so important, in fact, that if writers misspell even one word on a letter of application, they probably will not get an interview.

Although having a spell checker on a computer is a great help, it is a mixed blessing. The spell checker cannot recognize an error such as *affect* for *effect*, causing the writer to appear careless. Lesson 26, however, will help you gain a command of these most common spelling errors.

PART 4 PRETEST

Select the correct form from the choices given in parentheses.

1. It is (A. *too*, B. *to*) early to leave. _____

2. (A. *There*, B. *Their*) decision to spend money was criticized. _____

3. Interest rates had remained (A. *stationary*, B. *stationery*). _____

4. (A. *You're*, B. *Your*) doing really well on the task. _____

5. The strike will (A. *effect*, B. *affect*) the air travel industry. _____

6. We planned (A. *to*, B. *too*) meet them later. _____

7. (A. *It's*, B. *Its*) a long way to travel. _____

8. I don't know (A. *whose*, B. *who's*) tape this is. _____

9. Do not stand up, or you will (A. *loose*, B. *lose*) your change. _____

10. The (A. *principal*, B. *principle*) did not disregard the regulations. _____

11. (A. *Choose*, B. *Chose*) the correct form. _____

12. I would rather read (A. *than*, B. *then*) write. _____

13. She is a person of high (A. *principals*, B. *principles*). _____

14. I gave my (A. *personal*, B. *personnel*) opinion. _____

15. It was Daniel Boone's custom to sleep outdoors in any (A. *weather*, B. *whether*). _____

16. Their (A. *advice*, B. *advise*) was to visit the school while the students were studying. _____

17. He could not find out what (A. *affect*, B. *effect*) his letter had on the interviewer. _____

18. (A. *It's*, B. *Its*) cover was misplaced. _____

19. My sense of humor (A. *desserted*, B. *deserted*) me. _____

20. Did the low unemployment rate (A. *effect*, B. *affect*) the number of applications? _____

Spelling Demons

Thirty spelling demons.

Lesson 26 includes the most commonly misspelled words not recognized by the computer. Some have mnemonic devices to help you remember. Study these words, use them in sentences, look them up in other sources, and do everything you can to assure your grasp of these thirty demons.

The First Fifteen Spelling Demons

1. **to** The preposition and infinitive are spelled *to*. *To* Toledo; *to* run. "Try *to* improve your handwriting."

2. **too** *Too* is an adverb meaning excessively or also. "We were there *too*."

3. **two** *Two* is a number (2). Associate *two* with *twice*. "They were *two* miles from home."

4. **their** (*Their* is the possessive, the owner, the *heir*. He is the *heir* to all their possessions.) "*Their* credit rating is good."

5. **there** *There* is an adverb. (*Here* and *there*) "*There* were many indications of the success of the project."

6. **stationary** *Stationary* is an adjective pertaining to a fixed station. (A stationary part stays.) "The desks were *stationary*."

7. **stationery** *Stationery* refers to writing materials. (Letters are of paper.) "They bought envelopes at the *stationery* store."

8. **you're** The apostrophe replaces the *a* in the expression *you are*. "*You're* usually right."

9. **your** Never use an apostrophe with the possessive adjective. "It should not affect *your* standing."

10. **it's** The apostrophe replaces the *i* in the expression *it is*. "*It's* a clever idea."

11. **its** Never use an apostrophe with the possessive adjective. "The town is proud of *its* university."

12. **whose** *Whose* is the possessive form of *who* or *which*. "*Whose* records are these?"

13. **who's** *Who's* is the contraction for *who* and *is*, the apostrophe replacing the *i* in the expression *who is*. "*Who's* going?"

14. **loose** *Loose* means not confined, slack. (A loose tooth.) "The binding was *loose*."

15. **lose** *Lose* means the opposite of to keep or gain. (Please do not move, or I will lose.) "Be careful not to *lose* your way."

Check Your Understanding of the First Fifteen Spelling Demons

In each sentence, circle the correctly spelled word enclosed in parentheses.

1. I (*too*, *to*) wish to dispute your (*two*, *too*) statements.

2. To take one would be (*too*, *to*) uncharitable.

3. (*Their*, *They're*) writing many letters.

4. (*It's*, *Its*) an ingenious invention.

5. The office manager ordered new (*stationary*, *stationery*).

6. The instructor found (*your*, *you're*) writing commendable.

7. (*Whose*, *Who's*) notebook is this?

8. If the balloon gets (*loose*, *lose*), you might (*lose*, *loose*) it.

Answers: 1. too/two 2. too 3. They're 4. It's 5. stationery 6. your 7. Whose 8. loose/lose

Fifteen More Spelling Demons

1. **principal** *Principal* means taking first place—highest in character or importance. (The princip*al* of a school is a p*al* to you.) "The *principal* idea was to begin early and leave early."

2. **principle** *Principle* means a primary truth or rule such as the *principles* of law and the *principle* of integrity. (The principle meaning a rule ends in *le* as rule does.) "It is the *principle* of the matter that counts."

3. **choose** Choose a goose. "They always *choose* the right answers."

4. **chose** Who chose those hose? "We *chose* the wrong color."

5. **than** *Than* is a conjunction. "I would rather walk *than* jog."

6. **then** *Then* is an adverb and carries with it the idea of time. "We gave our report; *then* we left for the meeting."

7. **personal** *Personal* means belonging to a *person*—peculiar to a person or his private concerns. "The candidate told of her many *personal* experiences."

8. **personnel** The word *personnel* pertains to a group of persons engaged in some enterprise. "The *personnel* of the company include several recent graduates."

9. **whether** *Whether* or not. "*Whether* or not they will attend is still not known."

10. **advice** *Advice* is a noun meaning counsel. (Adv*ice* about the *ice*) "The professor's *advice* was followed."

11. **advise** *Advise* is a verb meaning to inform. "We *advise* you not to buy it."

12. **affect** *Affect* is a verb and means to influence. This is not usually a noun. "The climate *affected* their health."

13. **effect** *Effect* is usually a noun. "The *effect* of her concern was obvious." Occasionally *effect* can be a verb, meaning to bring about. "I hope you will be able to *effect* a better relationship between the departments."

14. **desert** *Desert* means to leave or forsake. "The managers should not *desert* their employees." Desert can also refer to unoccupied land. "*Desert* soil is not usually conducive to abundant vegetation."

15. **dessert** *Dessert* is a fruit or confection served at the close of a meal. (It has two *s*'s like strawberry shortcake.) "The *dessert* was delicious!"

Check Your Understanding of Fifteen More Spelling Demons

In each sentence, circle the correctly spelled word enclosed in parentheses.

1. The (*principal*, *principle*) street runs north.

2. My brother is older (*than*, *then*) I am.

3. Last week, the students (*choose*, *chose*) to write career objectives.

4. The (*principal*, *principle*) of the school was a person of strong beliefs.

5. The admonition of the dean had a good (*affect*, *effect*).

6. All (*personnel*, *personal*) were present.

7. I decided not to order (*desert*, *dessert*).

8. (*Weather*, *Whether*) they pass or not depends upon their studying.

9. The instructor gave (*advice*, *advise*) to fifty students.

10. That statement is true, but it does not (*affect*, *effect*) the case.

Answers: 1. principal 2. than 3. chose 4. principal 5. effect 6. personnel 7. dessert 8. Whether 9. advice 10. affect

Sentences for Dictation

Study the words in the following sentences. You can have a friend dictate them, or you can learn to dictate them to yourself by reading them and then writing them down from memory. Your instructor may also use these sentences to check your progress. In any event, be sure you can spell and use the proper punctuation for the following sentences:

1. There stood their uncle.

2. They're writing on your stationery.

3. You're too tired to run; it's now two o'clock.

4. Its cover was misplaced.

5. Whose friend is losing business?

6. If it gets loose, you will lose it.

7. Who's going to complain about the personnel?

8. The principal's judgment was correct.

9. Not everybody's principles need improving.

10. Sue's advice did not affect their success.

11. He was advised not to take the lawyer's advice.

12. The dean's warning had a good effect.

13. It did not, however, affect their grades.

14. Tell me whether the weather is hot or cold.

15. Now is better than then or tomorrow.

The Absent-Minded Professor

Find four spelling errors. Cross out each incorrectly spelled word, and replace it with the correct one.

Apply It !

Professor Wilson's principle failing was her absent-mindedness. This often led her too misplace articles necessary to her teaching. One day as she and another professor were walking on campus, Professor Wilson suddenly stopped, looked perplexed, and said to her friend, "Why, my notes for today's lecture have disappeared. If I don't find those notes, I will disappoint my class."

"What is that in your hand?" her colleague asked.

"Copies of the law review I just picked up at the printing center," she replied. "My notes were in a separate envelope of about the same size."

"Wait a minute," said the other professor. With a knowing look, he went to the center and took an envelope from the top of the cabinet. This he than brought to Professor Wilson, saying, "Don't misplace these notes again."

Professor Wilson, happy at being relieved of her anxiety, seized the envelope and said gratefully, "Thank you so much. I promise never to loose them again—at least not today."

IMPROVE YOUR VOCABULARY
Roots and Prefixes

MAL: bad, evil

Examples

A *malefactor* is any kind of *evil*-doer.

Malicious gossip springs from ill, or *bad*, will.

A *malady* is any disease or "*badness*" of the body.

To *malign* a person's character is to say *bad* things about him.

Malevolent is wishing *evil* or harm to others.

Vocabulary Check

For each sentence, fill each blank with an appropriate word from the list at the right.

1. A poor diet can lead to_____.
2. The disease _____ was once thought to be due to bad air.
3. To _____ people's characters is to say bad things about them.
4. People who complain a great deal are _____.
5. A condition that is harmful as opposed to being benign is considered _____.

malaria
malcontents
malign
malignant
malnutrition

Noun Plurals

At first glance, it might not seem important to study noun plurals. Yet almost everyone can profit from a review of this subject since plurals can be confusing. Although you may occasionally need to look up the correct form of a plural, Lesson 27 will help you be sure of writing correctly nouns that mean more than one.

27a The Plurals of Most Nouns

1. Form the plurals of most nouns by adding *s* or *es* to the singular:

   letter, letters   check, checks   bus, buses

2. Form the plurals of nouns ending in *y* preceded by a consonant by substituting *i* for *y* and adding *es*:

   policy, policies   company, companies   reply, replies

3. Add *s* only for nouns ending in *y* preceded by a vowel:

 key, keys   bay, bays   attorney, attorneys

4. When a word ends with *f* or *fe*, sometimes *s* is added. Sometimes the *f* is changed to *ves*.

 thief, thieves   half, halves   knife, knives

5. Usually add only *s* when a word ends with *o*.

 piano, pianos   portfolio, portfolios   stereo, stereos

6. Add *es* to the following:

 potato, potatoes tomato, tomatoes hero, heroes echo, echoes

These words are spelled correctly either way:

 mosquitoes, mosquitos tornadoes, tornados cargoes, cargos

Check Your Understanding of the Plural of Most Nouns
In each sentence, circle the correct word enclosed in parentheses.

1. Many birds live in the (*marshs*, *marshes*).

2. Two well-known (*cities*, *citys*) are New York and Boston.

3. Some of the (*companys*, *companies*) closed early.

4. She made sure that (*potatos*, *potatoes*) were on the menu.

Answers. 1. marshes 2. cities 3. companies 4. potatoes

Note: Use the same form for both singular and plural for some nouns.

 deer *is*, deer *are*   series *is*, series *are*   species *is*, species *are*

27b Compound Nouns
Form the plural of most compound nouns by making the main part of the noun plural.

 father-in-law, fathers-in-law
 account payable, accounts payable
 brother-in-law, brothers-in-law
 editor in chief, editors in chief

Form the plural at the end of hyphenated compounds not containing a main word and compound nouns consisting of one word:

trade-in, trade-ins   cupful, cupfuls
cure-all, cure-alls   run-through, run-throughs

Check Your Understanding of Compound Nouns

In each sentence, circle the correct word enclosed in parentheses.

1. Several (*bills of lading, bill of ladings*) were misplaced.

2. Several (*commander in chiefs, commanders in chief*) were mentioned.

3. She always praised her (*sons-in-law, son-in-laws*).

4. The participants were able to view both (*chiefs of staff, chief of staffs*).

5. The two (*editors in chief, editor in chiefs*) did answer their e-mail.

6. Both of my (*sister-in-laws, sisters-in-law*) told of their travels.

7. The family had many (*get-togethers, gets-together*).

8. Several (*attorneys-at-law, attorney-at-laws*) arranged to meet.

Answers: 1. bills of lading 2. commanders in chief 3. sons-in-law 4. chiefs of staff 5. editors in chief 6. sisters-in-law 7. get-togethers 8. attorneys-at-law

27c Proper Nouns

Form the plural of proper names by adding *s*.

Jenny   Jennys
Mr. and Mrs. Woodson   the Woodsons
Mr. and Mrs. McGovern   the McGoverns

If the last sound will not easily unite with *s*, add *es*:

Phyllis   Phyllises
Mr. and Mrs. Welsh   the Welshes
Mr. and Mrs. Jones   the Joneses

Note: Do not use apostrophes with proper names.

Incorrect: The Taylors' live on Forest Street.
Correct: The Taylors live on Forest Street.

Check Your Understanding of Proper Nouns

In each sentence, circle the correct word enclosed in parentheses.

1. There are two (*Roberts, Robert's*) in class.

2. There are also three (*Charles, Charleses*) in the class.

3. She had not realized that there were several (*James, Jameses*) in the department.

4. There are two (*Mahoney's, Mahoneys*) in the group.

5. She had several (*Davis's, Davises*) on her list.

Answers: 1. Roberts 2. Charleses 3. Jameses 4. Mahoneys 5. Davises

Note: To form the plurals of most abbreviations, add an *s* alone: IOUs, HMOs, DVDs. To form the plural of lower case letters followed by periods, use the apostrophe if adding *s* alone would be confusing: c.o.d.'s.

27d Nouns of Foreign Origin

Form the plurals of nouns of foreign origin in various ways:

Singular	Plural
alumna	alumnae (feminine)
alumnus	alumni (masculine)*
fungus	fungi (or funguses)
agendum (rarely used)	agenda
bacterium	bacteria
datum (rarely used)	data
erratum	errata
medium	media (or mediums)
memorandum	memoranda
criterion	criteria
phenomenon	phenomena
analysis	analyses
antithesis	antitheses
diagnosis	diagnoses
parenthesis	parentheses

Note: If there is one male in the group, it becomes a group of alumni.

Check Your Understanding of Nouns of Foreign Origin

In each sentence, circle the correct word enclosed in parentheses.

1. The (*alumnae*, *alumni*) of the coeducational college are meeting here.

2. The two women were (*alumnae*, *alumni*) of the college.

3. Mr. Green said that the shooting stars were wonderful (*phenomenon*, *phenomena*).

4. The (*criteria*, *criterion*) used were not rigid.

5. All the (*datum*, *data*) had not arrived in time for the report.

6. (*Parenthesis*, *Parentheses*) are used to set off an explanation or comment within a sentence.

7. The patient's (*diagnosis*, *diagnoses*) was not listed on the chart.

8. Some (*bacterium*, *bacteria*) are necessary for fermentation.

Answers: 1. alumni 2. alumnae 3. phenomena 4. criteria 5. data 6. Parentheses 7. diagnosis 8. bacteria

Sweet Potato Casserole

The following recipe has six errors. Find and correct them.

Mrs. Britney's Sweet Potato Casserole

4 medium sweet potatos
Vegetable oil spray
¼ teaspoonful nutmeg
2 tablespoonsful chopped walnuts
¼ cupful of orange juice

Cook whole sweet potatoes in boiling water 25 to 30 minutes or until tender. Meanwhile, preheat oven to 375 degrees. Lightly spray a 1-quart casserole dish with vegetable oil spray.

Remove potatoes from heat, and add cold water until potatoes are cooled slightly. Peel and mash. Add remaining ingredients, and mix thoroughly. Place in casserole dish, and bake uncovered 25 minutes.

Serve hot. Garnish with tomatos.

IMPROVE YOUR VOCABULARY
Roots and Prefixes

MANU, MAN: hand

Prefixes

a, *ab*, *abs*: from, away

Examples

An *amanuensis* is a secretary employed to copy *manuscripts* or to write letters from *hand*, or dictation.

A *man*acle is a *hand*cuff.

*Man*ual training gives education in the use of the *hands*.

When the word was invented, *manufacturing* was carried on entirely by *hand*.

Manumit is literally to "send a *hand*," to free from slavery.

Vocabulary Check

For each sentence, fill each blank with an appropriate word from the list at the right.

1. Most _____ today are keyed on the computer rather than directly written by hand.
2. A _____ is care of the hands and nails.
3. The fundamental meaning of _____ is to control with the hands.
4. To _____ is to operate or manage skillfully by means of the hands.
5. A _____ truth is so obvious that it seems to reach out and seize you by the hand.

manage
manicure
manifest
manipulate
manuscripts

Clearness is the fundamental quality of style, a quality so essential in every kind of writing that for want of it, nothing can atone.
—Hugh Blair, 1783

Style

Do You Make These Mistakes in Writing?

WRONG	RIGHT
Use fancy words to impress others.	Use simple, specific words.
Write wordy sentences.	Condense elements, and delete unnecessary words.
Present the same thought twice.	Eliminate sentences with the same thought unless for emphasis.
Write childish sentences.	Vary the length, beginnings, forms, and kinds of sentences.
Write skimpy paragraphs.	Supply sufficient details and particulars to support a topic sentence.
Compose difficult-to-read works.	Use the great principles of Unity, Coherence, and Force to write clearly and forcefully.

Clearness, clearness, clearness. Clearness *is* the prize in writing and is always the mark of a good style. Force, the ability to express ourselves in such a way as to make it likely our readers will remember what we have said, is also important.

Fortunately, you need to know only several principles—the great qualities of Unity, Coherence, and Force, or Emphasis—in order to be able to write in a good style. In the following lessons, you will learn how to apply these principles to improve your writing.

PART 5 PRETEST

In the space provided, write one of the following letters (A or B) to identify the more effective word or words in each sentence.

1. They (A. *initiated*, B. *started*) a cleanup campaign.   _____

2. Alberto (A. *disseminated*, B. *gave out*) the brochures.   _____

3. Your order will be sent (A. *without delay*, B. *by July 10*).   _____

4. Alicia is (A. *as steady as a rock,* B. *a reliable employee*).   _____

5. (A. *As per your request*, B. *As you requested*), we have prepared a new proposal.   _____

In the space provided, write A if the sentence is effective and B if the sentence is ineffective.

6. Being a CEO who managed a busy office.   _____

7. If a student is unable to attend the workshop, you are supposed to get a letter.   _____

8. The work is interesting, and the opportunities for advancement are good.   _____

9. The supervisor opened the letter; then he realized that it was addressed to someone else.   _____

10. Walking down the hall, a loud noise startled me.   _____

11. We only drove a mile.   _____

12. Having read the report, Ann made a list of questions.   _____

13. She found a dog in the car, which was dark brown with white spots.   _____

14. Alan likes both snowboarding and to ski.   _____

15. Officials, however, believe that the plan can work.   _____

16. You know that your efforts are appreciated by us.   _____

17. Jean said that she would stop by on the way home.   _____

18. There is not one of these letters that is clear and logical.   _____

19. The lock is broken, however, I think we can fix it.   _____

20. As it was just what I needed at this time of the evening.   _____

Clear and Forceful Words

This lesson covers improving writing with clear and forceful words.

28a	Simple words.	*Write __send__ rather than __transmit__.*
28b	Specific words.	*Use __sparrow__ rather than __bird__.*
28c	Outdated expressions.	*Avoid "at the end of the day."*
28d	Negative and offensive words.	*Avoid "You made a bad mistake."*

Words do make a difference. If we *apprise* our readers of the details instead of *giving* them the details, we make it harder for them to grasp our meaning. Lesson 28 will help you to think about the words you use and to strive for clear and forceful words—clear enough for others to understand what you mean and forceful enough to take effect.

28a Simple Words

For clearness, use a simple word rather than a fancy or pretentious one. Use *help* instead of *facilitate*, *fear* rather than *apprehension*, *use* in place of *utilize*, and *truth* instead of *veracity*. Ask yourself, "Would I use this word in conversation?" If not, find a more natural one.

Pretentious: The judge *terminated* the meeting immediately.
Simple: The judge *ended* the meeting immediately.

Pretentious Word	Simple Word
initiate	start
purchase	buy
assist	help

Check Your Understanding of Simple Words

In each sentence, circle the more simple word or words enclosed in parentheses.

1. The biologist performed the experiment with (*alacrity*, *eagerness*).

2. Filing online will (*expedite*, *speed up*) your tax refund.

3. The manager (*sent*, *dispatched*) the message to the president of the company.

4. Ramona (*exhibited*, *showed*) the new laptops to the parents.

5. The school board plans to (*terminate*, *end*) our bus service.

6. I did receive (*remuneration*, *payment*) for my work.

7. Did you (*ascertain*, *find out*) how many students are in your class?

8. We sent (*approximately*, *about*) four hundred e-mails.

Answers: 1. eagerness 2. speed up 3. sent 4. showed 5. end 6. payment 7. find out 8. about

28b Specific Words

For greater clarity and force, use a specific rather than a general word. A specific word is more definite and offers less chance for misunderstanding. It is also more likely to capture attention.

Precise Nouns. Use nouns that are precise and that show the reader exactly what you mean. *Flower*, for example, is less specific than *larkspur*, *daisy*, *rose*, *pansy*, or *tulip*. *Tree* is more general than *oak*, *pine*, *ash*, *maple*, or *tupelo*. And *anger* is less precise than *resentment*, *animosity*, *indignation*, *wrath*, *fury*, or *rage*.

Vivid Verbs. Use verbs that call up vivid images. As you've learned, linking verbs merely join nouns to their complements, but action verbs call up images. The more specific the action verb, the more vivid is the image. The general word *say*, for instance, is not so vivid or forceful as the more specific words *contend*, *remark*, *assert*, *announce*, *tell*, *maintain*, *affirm*, *state*, *respond*, and *answer*.

Varied Adjectives. Use varied and meaningful adjectives. Make sure you are not relying on certain overworked ones, such as *good*, *bad*, *great*, *difficult*, and *fine*. There are at least sixty-five similar words that you could substitute for the adjective *good*. When you acquaint yourself with the most commonly used adjectives and synonyms for them, you will find it easy to choose meaningful, specific words.

Check Your Understanding of Specific Words

In each sentence, circle the more specific word or words enclosed in parentheses.

1. At Lancaster we stopped for (*lobster, lunch*).

2. Mr. Williams (*says, insists*) that he will leave.

3. It is unusual to find (*skyscrapers, tall buildings*) in earthquake country.

4. Ms. Thomas promised to send the report (*next Tuesday, soon*).

5. Homeward-bound lawyers (*poured, came*) out of the elevators.

6. I saw a (*dog, dachshund*) on my walk.

7. It was a (*good, comprehensive*) report.

8. They sent a (*bad, confusing*) evaluation.

Answers. 1. lobster 2. insists 3. skyscrapers 4. next Tuesday 5. poured 6. dachshund 7. comprehensive 8. confusing

28c Outdated Expressions

Avoid outdated expressions, also known as clichés, jargon, and trite expressions. These are expressions we have heard so often that we have grown tired of them. A group called the Plain English Campaign recently listed the clichés people around the world found most annoying. The most annoying are listed first with the others listed in the columns.

- At the end of the day

- At this moment in time

- The constant use of *like*, as if it were a form of punctuation

- With all due respect

24/7	Bear with me.	I hear what you're saying.
absolutely	blue-sky thinking	in terms of
address the issue	bottom line	It's not rocket science.
awesome	crack troops	literally
ballpark figure	glass half full	

Your writing will be stronger if you replace these wordy expressions with shorter, simpler ones.

Instead of	*Use*
as per your request	as you requested
at this point in time	now
for all intents and purposes	virtually
in a timely fashion	promptly
par for the course	typical

Check Your Understanding of Outdated Expressions

Underline each outdated or worn-out expression. If a sentence does not contain an outdated expression, write E for effective after it.

1. It was, like, the worst presentation I have ever heard.

2. Writers sometimes use more words than necessary to convey their meaning.

3. Megan came away from the meeting sadder but wiser.

4. He had a high regard for Ms. Brewster's knowledge of these matters.

5. Last but not least, the committee looked at absenteeism.

6. Getting information about benefits online is easier said than done.

7. Success comes from hard work and from enthusiasm about what you are doing.

8. Please be advised that the interest rates may change.

Answers. 1. like 2. effective 3. sadder but wiser 4. effective 5. Last but not least 6. easier said than done 7. effective 8. Please be advised that

28d Negative and Offensive Words

A word or two can offend a reader, contributing to a loss in goodwill for the writer or company. Suppose, for example, a salesperson wrote to a customer, "We cannot fill your order because you neglected to fill out the credit information." The customer might become angry and decide to buy from another company. In the following examples, note how choosing different words turns a sentence that might offend the reader into a professional-sounding one:

Negative: You failed to return the disk.
Improved: The disk was not enclosed.

Negative: We have just received your complaint.
Improved: We have just received your suggestion.

Check Your Understanding of Negative and Offensive Words

Underline each negative or offensive word or phrase. If a sentence does not contain a negative or offensive word or phrase, write E for effective after it.

1. No one has ever complained about our air conditioners before.

2. Please send a remittance to cover your invoice of April 6.

3. We are completely at a loss to understand your concern.

4. You never gave us the design.

5. To complete your order, we will need to know which color you prefer.

Answers: 1. No one has ever complained 2. effective 3. completely at a loss 4. never 5. effective

Word Games for Better Words

Fill in the blanks to replace each pretentious word with a simpler word or phrase.

Apply It !

transcend	r _ s e a b _ _ e	canine	d _ g
commence	b _ _ i n	prevarication	l _ e
objective	g o _ l	comprehend	u n _ _ r s t _ _ d

Fill in the blanks to replace each general word with more specific words.

cereal	o _ t m _ _ l , p _ f f e d r _ _ e
furniture	c h _ _ r , d _ _ k , b _ _ k c _ s e , b _ d
building	s c h _ _ l , h _ _ s e , g _ r _ g e , b _ r n

Match each outdated expression with a more effective choice by placing the correct letter in each blank.

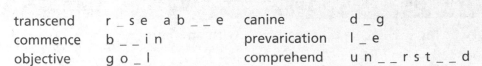

_____ 1. in the amount of   a. omit

_____ 2. it should be noted that   b. thank you for

_____ 3. this is to acknowledge   c. for

IMPROVE YOUR VOCABULARY
Roots and Prefixes

MIT, MISS: send, let go

Prefixes

com, *con*: with, together
dis: apart, not
e, *ex*: out
pre: before
re: again, back

Examples

The *commissariat* is the supply department of an army, which provides or *sends* food and supplies.

The student did not want to *commit*, or "*send forth with*," himself without more information.

A *missionary* is a person who is *sent* on a special mission.

A *missive* is a message or letter *sent* by one person to another.

Vocabulary Check

For each sentence, fill each blank with an appropriate word from the list at the right.

1. To _____ light is to send it out.
2. A _____ is a person who is sent on a special mission.
3. A conclusion is based on a _____ that comes or is "sent" before it.
4. To _____ a class is to send all the students away.
5. The statement "please _____" on a bill is a request for payment to be sent back to the vendor in exchange for goods received.

dismiss
emit
missionary
premise
remit

Lesson (29)

Unified Sentences

This lesson covers guidelines to make sentences unified.

29a	Complete sentences.	*Each day I had four classes. Each was forty-five minutes long.*
29b	Keeping to one point of view.	*Work quickly, and then close up the office.*
29c	Using only related ideas in a sentence.	*My composition is original, and I consequently should get a good grade.*
29d	Including necessary words.	*Erik heard <u>that</u> the noise had been caused by a broken piston.*
29e	Avoiding run-on sentences.	*We think so; however, we are not sure.*

To have unity—a oneness of thought—a sentence must express one central idea. This central idea may be accompanied by a subordinate idea, but you need to place all the parts together to produce the effect of one thought. Lesson 29 will show you specific ways in which to make your sentences unified. These include writing complete sentences, keeping to one point of view, using only related ideas, including necessary words, and avoiding run-on sentences.

29a Complete Sentences

Do not write a phrase or a clause as a sentence. Such an error—a sentence fragment—violates the fundamental rule that a sentence must be a complete statement with a subject and predicate.

To avoid this error, make sure you know the difference between a sentence and a phrase, a sentence and a dependent clause, and a noun or pronoun and a verbal ending in –*ing*. Although you learned these basics in Part 1, review them frequently to be sure you have a thorough understanding of the sentence.

Phrase Used as a Sentence

Incorrect: Evan was tired. *Having been up all night.*
Correct: Evan was tired, *having been up all night.*

Dependent Clause Used as a Sentence

Incorrect: He knows little about computers. *Although he has read several books on the subject.*
Correct: He knows little about computers, *although he has read several books on the subject.*

Noun or Pronoun and Verbal Ending in –*ing* Used as a Sentence

Incorrect: Money meant little to Danielle. Her chief interest being the development of a business program.
Correct: Money meant little to Danielle, her chief interest being the development of a business program.

Check Your Understanding of Complete Sentences

Attach each incomplete sentence to a complete sentence. If both sentences are complete, write C after them.

1. Please look at this spreadsheet. It contains all the figures.

2. Tien got the part. Even though she did not speak loudly enough.

3. Many students go to college and live at home. Combining the advantages of both.

4. Carla sent the memo. Having made all the changes.

5. The trustees rejected the plan. The reason they gave was a lack of funds.

6. Having said what he wanted. George ended the letter.

29b Keeping to One Point of View

All parts of the sentence should move in the same direction. Avoid any shifts, especially in the subject, as the following example demonstrates:

Original: If *one* works hard, *you* can accomplish much.
Improved: If *you* work hard, *you* can accomplish much.

Check Your Understanding of Keeping to One Point of View

Correct each sentence that does not keep to one point of view. If the sentence does not need changing, write E after it.

1. If one practices enough, you can learn to key.

2. When you are buying online, you should take some precautions.

3. Nick rushed to the airport, and the plane was boarded by him.

4. A student can apply for a Stafford Loan if you need money for college.

29c Using Only Related Ideas in a Sentence

Unity requires that the ideas in a sentence be related. Defects in unity may be corrected in one of two ways.

The first is to place the unrelated statements in different sentences.

Original: Jane will visit us next month, and she works as a reporter.
Improved: Jane will visit us next month. She works as a reporter.

The second is to subordinate one statement to another.

Improved: Jane, who will visit us next month, works as a reporter.
Improved: Jane, a reporter, will visit us next month.

Check Your Understanding of Using Only Related Ideas in a Sentence

Revise each sentence that does not use related ideas properly. For sentences 1–3, place the unrelated statements in different sentences. For sentences 4–6, subordinate one statement to another. If a sentence is effective, write E after it.

1. John is studying history, and I do not expect to go to Egypt.

2. Chemistry is my most difficult subject, and the semester ends Friday.

3. The informal speaker is an entertainer, and the formal speaker is an instructor.

4. Ms. Shea is a special education teacher, and she described the accident.

5. Hector had 20 hours of training, and he works as a mediator.

6. Rina spoke on global trade patterns, and she just returned from Japan.

Answers. 1. John is studying history. I do not expect to go to Egypt. 2. Chemistry is my most difficult subject. The semester ends Friday. 3. effective 4. Ms. Shea, a special education teacher, described the accident. 5. Hector, who had 20 hours of training, works as a mediator. 6. Rina, who just returned from Japan, spoke on global trade patterns.

29d Including Necessary Words

Always include the subject and any other necessary words, such as verbs, articles, and prepositions, the omission of which could affect the unity of the sentence.

Original: Waiting to hear from you.
Improved: I will wait to hear from you.

The word *that* can often be left out of a sentence. Sometimes, though, it is needed for clarity or to keep the sentence from being misread.

Original: Mr. Jones stated the purpose of his book was to teach Web site design.
Improved: Mr. Jones stated *that* the purpose of his book was to teach Web site design.

Check Your Understanding of Necessary Words

For each sentence, supply any missing word that could affect the unity of the sentence. If a sentence is effective, write E after it.

1. Julia has interest and regard for the work of her associates.

2. He has been and always will be a faithful supporter.

3. Will telephone you at the end of July.

4. The student's skill in programming was equal to that of an expert.

5. We believe the study should be repeated each year.

29e Avoiding Run-On Sentences

The most serious writing error is the run-on sentence. Such an error consists of joining two sentences with a comma or running them together with no punctuation. A run-on sentence, however, is not so much an error in punctuation as it is a transgression against the idea of what a sentence is.

Run-on: We had that experience once, we do not want it again.

Run-on: We had that experience once we do not want it again.

There are three ways to correct a run-on sentence. You can make it into two sentences, separate the two parts of the sentence with a semicolon, or add a comma and a conjunction:

Correct: We had that experience once. We do not want it again.

Correct: We had that experience once; we do not want it again.

Correct: We had that experience once, and we do not want it again.

Check Your Understanding of Run-On Sentences

Correct each run-on sentence with a semicolon. If a sentence is correct, write C after it.

1. Gina liked *Pacific Crossing*, Kate preferred *The Endless Steppe*.

2. In the past, however, the company paid dividends.

3. At first they were annoyed, then they saw the humor of the situation.

4. Please take this brochure, it describes our products.

5. We enjoyed the curry, still we have had better.

Apply It !

A Matching Exercise

The following sentences lack unity. Match each defective sentence to the type of error it contains. If a sentence is correct, make a check mark in the space provided.

_____ 1. I have written two letters. One to the president and one to the vice president.

_____ 2. Their office is located in Chicago, and they recently approved a new punctuation pamphlet.

_____ 3. They were concerned about punctuation errors, therefore, they sent a memo to all employees.

_____ 4. Errors, though, kept showing up in company documents.

_____ 5. The director of communications wrote the pamphlet, an associate designed it.

_____ 6. The director was new, and he asked that all employees study the pamphlet.

_____ 7. One manager, however, replied her associates did not need the new guides.

_____ 8. She said that if one proofreads carefully, he or she will find any errors.

_____ 9. Finally, the director devised a reward system.

_____ 10. She awarded points for every correctly punctuated document. Points that could be used to purchase items from a gift catalog.

a. Incomplete sentence

b. More than one point of view

c. Unrelated ideas in one sentence

d. Sentence lacking a necessary word

e. Run-on sentence

IMPROVE YOUR VOCABULARY
Roots and Prefixes

PEND, POND, PEN: weigh, hang, weigh in a balance

Prefixes

ad (*ap*): to, at
com: together
dis: apart, not
e, ex: out, out of

Examples

An *appendage* is attached to, or *hangs on*, something else.

An *appendix* is something attached to the end, or *hung* to it.

A *compendium* pulls, or *weighs*, material *together* and summarizes it.

Employees in a *dispensary weigh* out drugs.

To *expend* money is to spend it, or *weigh* it *out*.

Vocabulary Check

For each sentence, fill each blank with an appropriate word from the list at the right.

1. A person who has a _____ for chocolate leans toward eating it.
2. When employees are _____ for their work, they are paid an amount considered equivalent to their services.
3. A _____ is a person who relies, or leans, on another person for support.
4. To _____ money is to weigh it out in exchange for goods or services.
5. To _____ a file to an e-mail is to attach it.

append
compensated
dependent
penchant
spend

Lesson 30

Clear Sentences

This lesson covers suggestions for writing clear sentences.		
30a	**Dangling modifiers.**	*Walking to town, the train could be seen pulling into the depot.*
30b	**Parallel structure.**	*Annie likes swimming, skiing, and to play lacrosse.*
30c	**Illogical order.**	*Mr. Akita gave the bids to the committee on the roof.*

Dangling modifiers, inconsistent wording, and misplaced words are among the most distracting usage errors. In Lesson 30, you will learn to recognize these problems and avoid them.

30a Dangling Modifiers

A dangling modifier is a modifier that, agreeing with nothing, dangles in the air. A modifier dangles when it refers to no word or the wrong word in the sentence.

> *Original*: Stepping into the office, the disk was seen by the manager.
> (Did the *disk* step into the office?)
> *Improved*: Stepping into the office, the manager saw the disk.

Original: Upon entering the school, every defect was noted.
Improved: Upon entering the school, I noted every defect.

Check Your Understanding of Dangling Modifiers

Rewrite any sentence that contains a dangling modifier. If the sentence is effective, write E after it.

1. Planning the meeting, an agenda was put together by Ralph.

2. By running this software, viruses can be detected.

3. When copyedited, you may have the paper for keying.

4. In speaking to his instructor, Steve learned what he needed to study.

5. Having read your résumé, you are well qualified.

6. On entering the building, we saw a spacious hall.

Answers. 1. Planning the meeting, Ralph put together an agenda. 2. By running this software, you can detect viruses. 3. When copyedited, your paper will be ready for keying. 4. effective 5. Having read your résumé, I can see that you are well qualified. 6. effective

30b Parallel Structure

Ideas that are parallel in thought should be parallel in structure. In the following examples, note how matching adjectives with adjectives and phrases with phrases makes each sentence read better.

Original: Dolphins are *friendly, social*, and *they have intelligence*.
Improved: Dolphins are *friendly, social*, and *intelligent*.

Original: Andy prefers *taking the subway* to *a car*.
Improved: Andy prefers *taking the subway* to *driving a car*.

Original: The applicant had *a neat appearance, a cooperative attitude,* and *her personality was attractive*.
Improved: The applicant had *a neat appearance, a cooperative attitude,* and *an attractive personality*.

You can recognize ideas that should be parallel because they are linked by a conjunction, a connecting word such as *to*, or a pair of conjunctions such as *neither/nor* or *not only/but also*.

Check Your Understanding of Parallel Structure.

In each sentence, rewrite any element that is not parallel. If the items in the sentence are parallel, write E after it.

1. Mr. Brown's reports are clear, concise, and we find them absorbing.

2. For Ada, directing is more rewarding than to be an actor.

3. He is wise, witty, and cheerful.

4. To promise is easy; performing is more difficult.

5. The house was large, beautiful, and well furnished.

6. Alexa not only plays the violin but also the cello.

Answers. 1. Mr. Brown's reports are clear, concise, and absorbing. **2.** For Ada, directing is more rewarding than acting. **3.** effective **4.** To promise is easy; to perform is more difficult. **5.** effective **6.** Alexa plays not only the violin but also the cello.

30c Illogical Order

Related words should be placed as close together as possible.

Original: He had a scanner in his office that had been his supervisor's.

Improved: In his office, he had a scanner that had been his supervisor's.

Place words such as *only*, *almost*, *just*, *even*, and *hardly* immediately before the words they modify.

Original: I *only* deducted $50 from your paycheck.

Improved: I deducted *only* $50 from your paycheck.

Check Your Understanding of Illogical Order

In each sentence, move any element that is not placed logically to a better location. If a sentence is arranged logically, write E after it.

1. Jordi bought a t-shirt at the airport that was half price.

2. I only sent the article to one magazine.

3. He pointed out birds for the guests in the trees.

4. Eric had talked only a minute when the bell rang.

5. Jenny even checks the folders on weekends.

Note: Make sure your reader knows who is speaking. Mistakes like the following are often made even by good writers. Be especially careful when using *he*, *she*, and *it*.

Original: Luis told Brian that he had made an error. (*Who* made the error, Luis or Brian?)

Improved: Luis said, "Brian, you made an error."

Original: Tom's accountant quit during his busiest season. (*Whose* season was busy, Tom's or his accountant's?)

Improved: During Tom's busiest season, his accountant quit.

Our National Parks

Correct dangling modifiers, words that are not parallel, and words that are not in a logical order. If a sentence is effective, write E after it.

Apply It

1. Olympic National Park has glacier-capped mountains, rainforests, and it has old-growth trees.

2. We only had to wait ten minutes to see Old Faithful erupt.

3. When visiting Gettysburg, President Lincoln's famous speech came to mind.

4. At Carlsbad Caverns, we watched 300,000 bats dive into a cave while eating pancakes.

5. At Lassen Volcanic National Park, every type of volcano on Earth can be seen.

6. Her goals were to hike the Appalachian Trail and visiting Mount Rushmore.

7. As a student volunteer, you can dig for fossils in Badlands National Park.

8. At Assateague Island, we not only glimpsed wild horses but also sika deer.

9. While snorkeling at Everglades National Park, three manatees were seen.

10. Emma told Julie that she might like to see Devils Tower.

IMPROVE YOUR VOCABULARY
Roots and Prefixes

PLIC, PLI: fold, tangle

Prefixes

> *ad* (*ac*): to
> *com*: together
> *e*, *ex*: out, out of
> *im* (*in*): in, on, into
> *sub*: under

Examples

> An *accomplice* is a partner in crime, a person literally *folded* into it.
>
> *Explicit* instructions are clearly stated or *unfolded*.
>
> To *implicate* someone in a crime is to show the person is involved or *tangled* in it.
>
> An *implicit* wish is understood but not expressed; it is "*folded in.*"
>
> *Supplication* is a humble request or prayer, often made on bended or *folded* knees.

Vocabulary Check

For each sentence, fill each blank with an appropriate word from the list at the right.

1. Clay is _____ because it can be folded or bent easily.
2. _____, a partnership in wrongdoing, is literally a folding together.
3. A _____ problem is tangled and difficult to solve.
4. To _____ products in a store window is to unfold them to view.
5. To _____ is to suggest something without stating it directly.

complicated
complicity
display
imply
pliable

Forceful Sentences

This lesson covers suggestions for writing forceful sentences.

31a	**Placing important words in emphatic positions.**	*The accepted time is <u>now</u>.*
31b	**Varying the beginnings of sentences.**	*Slowly, the clock ticked away the seconds.*
31c	**Avoiding choppiness.**	*The storm, which lasted eight hours, battered the coast.*
31d	**Using active verbs.**	*Sarah won the race.*
31e	**Being concise.**	*My uncle, a writer, lives in California.*

With some effort, most of us can conquer the subject of clearness. What we really need to find out is how to write with force. In Lesson 31, we can learn to do this—and get our writing read and acted upon in a favorable way.

31a Placing Important Words in Emphatic Positions

Readers pay the most attention to the beginning and end of sentences, especially the end. Consequently, to give force or emphasis to important words, you should place them first or last.

Original:	It is probably true that *eating right* is the most important step you can take for good health.
Improved:	*Eating right* is probably the most important step you can take for good health.
Improved:	Probably the most important step you can take for good health is *to eat right*.

Not all sentences can be arranged to begin and end with important words. Many are too short and simple. In others, the word order cannot be changed. Very little can be done, for example, with a sentence like "Our task has been completed."

Note: Parenthetical expressions like *however*, *therefore*, and *nevertheless* should appear early in the sentence, preferably between the subject and the verb. So should expressions like *in my opinion*, *I think*, and *it seems to me*.

Original:	*However*, the fax arrived the next morning.
Improved:	The fax, *however*, arrived the next morning.

Check Your Understanding of Placing Important Words in Emphatic Positions

Rewrite each sentence that does not have important words in emphatic positions. If a sentence does not need improvement, write E after it.

1. Speedwriting, for instance, is a useful skill.

2. Natalie's plan is the one we should use, I think.

3. Our affluence depends, largely, upon the cooperation of capital and labor.

4. I believe that Rachel is our best engineer.

5. There are several factors that contributed to the accident.

Answers. 1. effective 2. Natalie's plan, I think, is the one we should use. 3. effective 4. Rachel, I believe, is our best engineer. 5. Several factors contributed to the accident.

31b Varying the Beginnings of Sentences

To add interest to your writing, vary the beginnings of sentences. Start with an adverb, a prepositional phrase, a verbal phrase, or a clause. Some authorities suggest putting something before the subject in a third to a half of your sentences.

Original:	Rico shut off the power *immediately*.
Forceful:	*Immediately*, Rico shut off the power.
Original:	I have worked as a consultant *for the past three years*.
Forceful:	*For the past three years*, I have worked as a consultant.

Check Your Understanding of Varying the Beginnings of Sentences

Rewrite each sentence to vary the beginning.

1. The firm closed its downtown office reluctantly.

2. Four members left the meeting as soon as the chairperson finished her remarks.

3. Protesters across the street waved their signs and shouted.

4. George left the room, carrying the tray.

5. The game was postponed because of the weather.

Answers. 1. Reluctantly, the firm closed its downtown office. **2.** As soon as the chairperson finished her remarks, four members left the meeting. **3.** Across the street, protesters waved their signs and shouted. **4.** Carrying the tray, George left the room. **5.** Because of the weather, the game was postponed.

Note: Here are some other ways of varying sentences.

Length: Use a mixture of short and long sentences. Try to limit your longest sentences to 20 words.

Forms: In addition to simple sentences, use compound and complex sentences.

Compound:	Carrie brought apples, and Ian brought cider.
Complex:	Since changing our system, we have handled many more calls.

Kinds: Interrogative, exclamatory, and imperative (command) sentences are usually more emphatic than declarative sentences.

> Is it necessary to tell everything about the incident?
> What a tragedy this is!
> Please close the door.

31c Avoiding Choppiness

Writers sometimes use too many short, simple sentences in a row. The result is choppy writing.

Original:	Dean Travis will visit the college on Friday, February 11. He will leave on Saturday, February 12. He will be staying at the Statler Hotel.
Improved:	Dean Travis will visit the college on Friday, February 11, and will leave on Saturday, February 12. He will be staying at the Statler Hotel.

Choppy writing can be avoided by combining sentences with related ideas and by subordinating less important elements to more important ones.

Original:	Professor Smith is an instructor at the college. He is our faculty adviser.
Improved:	Professor Smith, an instructor at the college, is our faculty adviser.

Check Your Understanding of Choppy Sentences

Revise the following choppy sentences.

1. Aaron collected the ballots. Kylie checked them.

2. Mr. Scott drafted the memo. He sent a copy to all the managers.

3. Karen has a small yard. Still she grows many flowers in it.

4. The plan was over budget. No one said so, though.

5. During a lunar eclipse, the moon is full. It passes through the umbra. The umbra is the darkest part of Earth's shadow.

Answers. 1. Aaron collected the ballots, and Kylie checked them. 2. Mr. Scott drafted the memo and sent a copy to all the managers. 3. Although Karen has a small yard, she grows many flowers in it. 4. The plan was over budget, yet no one said so. 5. During a lunar eclipse, the full moon passes through the umbra, the darkest part of Earth's shadow.

31d Using Active Verbs

A verb is **active** when the subject performs the action.

> The <u>committee</u> *wrote* the report.
> <u>Malcolm</u> *snipped* the two wires.

With a **passive verb**, the subject is acted upon.

> The <u>report</u> *was written* by the committee.
> The two <u>wires</u> *were snipped* by Malcolm.

Active verbs are direct, clear, and vigorous, and they make for concise sentences. When possible, therefore, use active verbs to make your writing more forceful.

This is not to say that you should never use passive verbs. Passive verbs are useful when the doer of the action is not known or not important or when you wish to show that the subject is being acted upon.

> Banks are closed on holidays.
> The checks were mailed on Friday.
> The bill was opposed by two-thirds of the members.

Check Your Understanding of Active Verbs

Make each sentence more forceful by substituting active verbs for passive ones. If the sentence is effective, write E after it.

1. A salad bar and sandwiches made to order are offered by the cafeteria.

2. Character is revealed by actions.

3. We dropped the subject.

4. The contract was approved by our attorney.

5. Three parked cars were sideswiped by the bus.

Answers. 1. The cafeteria offers a salad bar and sandwiches made to order. 2. Actions reveal character. 3. effective. 4. Our attorney approved the contract. 5. The bus sideswiped three parked cars.

31e Being Concise

The fewer number of words used to express an idea, the more clearly the idea can stand out. Delete every word that does not add to the meaning of your writing, and use the most expressive words possible. Do not present the same thought twice unless you want to emphasize it. These techniques will help make your sentences concise:

Omit unnecessary words. Unnecessary words can occupy from a fourth to a fifth of a message. Such words can include *there* and *it*; adjectives, conjunctions, and adverbs; and even subjects and verbs.

Original:	There were many employees at the convention.
Improved:	Many employees were at the convention.
Original:	The best example we have is her report on wireless networks.
Improved:	The best example is her report on wireless networks.

Condense elements. When reviewing your writing, you will come upon sentence parts that can be shortened, or condensed. The following examples show how clauses can be reduced to phrases, appositives, and single words; phrases to single words; and compound sentences to compound predicates.

A Clause Into a Phrase

Clause:	She explained *how the furniture should be arranged.*
Phrase:	She explained *how to arrange the furniture.*

A Clause Into an Appositive

Clause:	Mr. Davis, *who is an accountant*, left early.
Appositive:	Mr. Davis, *an accountant*, left early.

A Clause Into a Word

Clause:	The chest contained a drawer that was made of cedar.
Word:	The chest contained a *cedar* drawer.

A Phrase Into a Word

Phrase:	He was a person *of great enthusiasm.*
Word:	He was an *enthusiastic* person.

A Compound Sentence Into a Compound Predicate

Making a compound sentence into a compound predicate is particularly effective. It is simply a matter of deleting the subject and any unnecessary punctuation.

Original: They searched the office, and then they investigated the reports.

Improved: They searched the office and then investigated the reports.

Remember that in a sentence with a compound predicate, the second verb does not have its own subject, and a comma therefore would be distracting.

Check Your Understanding of Conciseness

Rewrite each sentence that can be made more concise. If a sentence is effective, write E after it.

1. We should provide all the facts and then wait for the company to respond.

2. There is not one of these computers that works well.

3. When you reach a decision, please let us know.

4. The house that I live in is around the corner.

5. Ellen Li, who is the mayor's assistant, promised us results.

6. Jan unpacked the supplies, and she checked them against a list.

7. The office was built on a slope that overlooked a brook.

8. He worked for a period of three days on the exam.

9. Before I joined the staff, I studied the company's policies.

10. Keith fixed the printer to run automatically.

Answers: 1. effective **2.** Not one of these computers works well. **3.** When you decide, please let us know. **4.** My house is around the corner. **5.** Ellen Li, the mayor's assistant, promised us results. **6.** Jan unpacked the supplies and checked them against a list. **7.** The office was built on a slope overlooking a brook. **8.** He worked for three days on the exam. **9.** Before joining the staff, I studied the company's policies. **10.** effective

Improve a Letter

Read each version of the following letter. Then for each sentence, write A, B, C, or D to describe the principle that the improved sentence follows. Some sentences may have more than one improvement.

_____ Sentence 1	A. Put important words first or last.
_____ Sentence 2	B. Vary the beginnings of sentences.
_____ Sentence 3	C. Use active verbs.
_____ Sentence 4	D. Be concise.
_____ Sentence 5	
_____ Sentence 6	
_____ Sentence 7	

Original Letter

I am eager to join your team as a graphic designer after reading of your expansion.**1** I believe I have gained the qualifications you call for from my work as a freelance designer.**2**

I have completed design projects that included brochures, logos, and direct mail programs over the last two years.**3** I am considered to work well under pressure, and I am considered to communicate well with others.**4** I have enclosed my résumé and portfolio samples so that I can highlight my experience and background.**5**

The position described by you sounds interesting, and I would like the opportunity to talk with you about it.**6** I will call you sometime in the next two weeks to discuss whether it would be possible for us to meet.**7**

Improved Version

After reading of your expansion, I am eager to join your team as a graphic designer.**1** I have gained the qualifications you call for, I believe, from my work as a freelance designer.**2**

Over the last two years, I have completed design projects that included brochures, logos, and direct mail programs.**3** I am considered to work well under pressure and to communicate well with others.**4** To highlight my experience and background, I have enclosed my résumé and portfolio samples.**5**

The position you describe sounds interesting, and I would like the opportunity to talk with you about it.**6** I will call sometime in the next two weeks to discuss whether we can meet.**7**

IMPROVE YOUR VOCABULARY
Roots and Prefixes

PON, POS: lay, put, place

Prefixes

com: with, together
de: from, down
in (*im*): in, on, into, against
ob (*op*): against
pro: for, forth, forward

Examples

To *compose* is to *put together*.

A *composition* is a piece of writing, art, or music that someone has *put together*.

A *compound* consists of two or more elements *placed together*.

To *depose* is to *put down* or remove from office.

To *oppose* is to set or *place* yourself *against* something.

Vocabulary Check

For each sentence, fill each blank with an appropriate word from the list at the right.

1. When a person _____, he or she puts forward a certain idea.
2. A _____ is a railroad station, a place where passengers are let off or put down.
3. The _____ "puts upon" people in an effort to deceive them.
4. If you are _____ about something, your views are firmly set.
5. To _____ money means to put it into an account.

depot
deposit
imposter
positive
proposes

Lesson ③②

The Paragraph

This lesson covers important qualities of paragraphs.

32a **Unity.** A oneness, with all necessary facts included and all unnecessary ones excluded.

32b **Coherence.** A clearness achieved through logical order of the paragraph as well as through the use of transitional expressions.

32c **Emphasis.** The stressing of certain parts, usually the beginning and end, so that they stand out from the rest of the paragraph.

32d **Four kinds of paragraphs.** Narrative, descriptive, expository, and persuasive.

The paragraph is actually a whole composition, or theme, on a small scale. The relation between a paragraph and a theme consists in the fact that the paragraph presents the development of one of the ideas that go to make up the whole theme. In Lesson 32, you will learn how the principles of composition can help you learn to write effective paragraphs.

32a Unity

The principle of Unity requires that each paragraph be devoted to a single idea. The thoughts necessary to explain it should be grouped about this idea, and no thought that does not contribute to the explanation should be included. The principle of Unity, which requires that every paragraph be a unit, is the first requisite of all good writing.

Suggestions

Include all the necessary facts. Remember, facts are the core of composition. Make sure, therefore, that you have sufficient supporting details for your paragraphs.

Eliminate facts that do not belong. A sentence may belong to some other paragraph of your theme, or it may have no logical connection with any part of your work. Make sure, therefore, that you eliminate any facts that do not belong.

Use a topic sentence. A topic sentence states clearly what a paragraph is about. It aids the reader by providing the main point or idea of the paragraph. If you place a topic sentence at the beginning of your paragraph, every other sentence in the paragraph can add to it or explain it. In this paragraph, note how the topic sentence states the main idea, which is developed and supported in the sentences that follow.

> *The Egyptians have taught us many things.* They were excellent farmers. They knew about irrigation. They built temples that were afterward copied by the Greeks and that served as the earliest models for the churches in which we worship nowadays. They invented a calendar that proved such a useful instrument for the purpose of measuring time that it has survived with a few changes until today. But, most important of all, the Egyptians learned how to preserve speech for the benefit of future generations. They invented the art of writing.
>
> Hendrik Van Loon, *The Story of Mankind*

Summarize a paragraph with a sentence. Occasionally, you may place the topic sentence within the paragraph or at the end, or you may not have one at all. When you write a paragraph without a topic sentence, check it for unity by trying to think of a sentence that summarizes it. Unity of the paragraph exists only when you can summarize it in a single sentence. Study the following paragraph, which has no topic sentence, and the sentence that summarizes it:

213

Paragraph	Summary
Billions of dollars are spent every year on sales letters. Only one in six of these letters is ever read. Are yours among the successful ones? Did you know that you can double your business by making your letters more compelling to read?	You can increase your business by writing more forceful letters.

32b Coherence

Paragraphs must be clear. The term *coherence* (a sticking together) is often used to refer to the quality of clearness in paragraphs. Coherence is achieved by arranging the sentences of a paragraph in a logical order and by using transitional expressions, such as *however* and *therefore*, to connect ideas.

Suggestions

Arrange your sentences in a logical order. The details of a paragraph should be arranged in a clear and sensible way. A good choice is chronological order, the arrangement of events in the order of occurrence. Two other methods are from least important to most important and from known to unknown.

Use transitional expressions to connect ideas. Transitional expressions join sentences and paragraphs meaningfully and guide the reader in connecting ideas. Here are some examples of transitional expressions:

Addition	*Contrast*	*Result*	*Time*
also, too	although	accordingly	afterwards
besides	but	as a result	at last
finally	however	consequently	first, second, etc.
furthermore	nevertheless	for that reason	next
in addition	on the contrary	since	soon
next	though	therefore	then

In the following paragraph, notice how the underlined transitional expressions are used to link ideas:

We believe that the benefits of the proposed light rail system outweigh the disadvantages. The system will not serve some areas, <u>but</u> it will provide access to major downtown employers and businesses. <u>Although</u> setup will be expensive, we can pay for it with existing sales tax revenue and federal grants. <u>Consequently</u>, we recommend that the proposal be adopted.

32c Emphasis

Emphasis is the principle in which certain parts of a sentence, paragraph, or composition are stressed so that they stand out from the rest. As in the sentence, the beginning and end of the paragraph are the places that catch the reader's attention. This is one reason why paragraphs often begin with a topic sentence. The final sentence, then, gives the last word on the subject that the first sentence introduced.

In the writing of single paragraphs, the principle of Emphasis is of great importance. In the first words, readers learn what the subject is, and in the last words, they find out what the conclusion is. In the body, they learn the details of the paragraph.

Suggestion

If possible, place important sentences at the beginning and end of each paragraph. Reread the paragraph on the Egyptians in section 32a. Notice not only the topic sentence but also how the most important point is placed last: *They invented the art of writing.*

32d Four Kinds of Paragraphs

There are four kinds of composition: Narration, which tells a story; Description, which creates pictures; Exposition, which explains; and Persuasion, which argues.

The Narrative Paragraph

A narrative paragraph tells a story. Such a paragraph may stand alone, or it may be part of a series of paragraphs.

I was working backstage at a local dinner theatre when a movie company filming nearby called requesting extras to play mourners at a funeral the next day. We were told to dress well; consequently, I joined a crowd of extras the next day at the cemetery in a black dress, hose, and heels, even though the temperature was in the mid-90s. The scene took hours to shoot, and I was hot and exhausted. The day finally ended, and many months later, the movie was released. As I watched it, I recognized my blurred form for a split second, but it had vanished by the time I could tell my friends, "There I am!"

The Descriptive Paragraph

A descriptive paragraph presents one definite impression of a person, thing, or place. This unified impression results from the writer's choosing only those qualities that contribute to the one main impression.

The shark's form has been unchanged for about 100 million years. Its stream-lined body, tapered at both ends, moves in a side-to-side motion like those of other fish. Its skeleton, however, is made of cartilage rather than bone. The shark has five to seven gill slits on each side of its head. Its paired external nostrils are used only for smell, not for taking in oxygen. The shark is equipped with parallel rows of teeth. Tooth loss and replacement continue throughout its lifetime. Diverse in size, the species includes the largest known fish, the Whale shark, which may reach 45 feet in length, and the Dwarf shark, only 8–10 inches long.

The Expository Paragraph

In the expository paragraph, the writer's main purpose is to explain a fact or an idea. Above all, the paragraph must be clear. More than ever, the writer must exercise care in the selection and arrangement of the material.

Physical fitness includes a person's aerobic and muscular endurance, muscular strength, flexibility, and muscle/fat ratio. Aerobic endurance reflects how well a person's heart and lungs work to supply needed oxygen to the body during physical exertion. Muscle strength is reflected in the ability to repeat movements or hold a particular exercise position, as well as the amount of effort it takes to lift weights. When a person can use full range of motion to demonstrate muscle elasticity, this indicates flexibility. Body composition compares the ratio of fat to bone and muscle and is not measured on a bathroom scale.

The Persuasive Paragraph

The persuasive paragraph tries to convince someone of something. For example, its purpose may be to convince a voter to choose a certain candidate or to convince a customer to buy a product.

When your parents told you to "go out and play" when you were a child, did you think that they were trying to get rid of you? In fact, they were sending you on an important mission. Plato said, "It is the essential nature of man to play," and play is essential for our health. Through play, children grow into adults who have learned how to get along with others, develop their creative and physical abilities, and build problem-solving skills. Furthermore, adults should continue to play throughout their lifetimes by taking part in a variety of activities. Whether you enjoy participating in sports and games, visiting theme parks, going to movies and museums, or stopping at yard sales, you need to engage in a fair measure of play.

Write Effective Paragraphs

1. Make notes for a sketch of your own life or the life of a family member. You may use the following suggested topics or choose your own. For each paragraph, try to think of at least five details.

   Paragraph 1: Family or childhood
   Paragraph 2: Education
   Paragraph 3: Work
   Paragraph 4: Personal description

2. Choose two of the following topic sentences, and expand each into a paragraph. Try to think of at least five details to use in each paragraph.

   a. Last _____ was an unusually busy day for me.
   b. _____ is someone whom I really admire.
   c. Ownership of a car carries with it many responsibilities.
   d. I admit I have one or two minor faults.
   e. There are many ways of becoming well liked at work.
   f. Of all my studies, I have gained the most from _____.
   g. I will always remember the (day/time) that _____.
   h. There is no such thing as an uneducated person.
   i. Hurrying does not always save time.
   j. If I could change one thing about my college, I would change _____ .

3. Choose one of the following topics and write several paragraphs on it:

   • Compare a book you've read to a movie made from it.
   • Identify several habits that lead to success at work.
   • Explain how you learned to do something, such as skate or play hockey.
   • Describe a television program or programs that you enjoy.
   • Explain what you hope to get out of college.
   • Describe some steps that people can take for good health.
   • Describe a place or an event that is especially memorable for you.
   • Explain how to prepare for a job interview.

IMPROVE YOUR VOCABULARY
Roots and Prefixes

SPECT, SPIC: look at, see

Prefixes

circum: around
com, con: with, together
de: from, down
e, ex: out, out of, from
in: in, into
per: through

Examples

Circumspect investors *look around* before acting.

A *conspicuous* error is one that is easily *seen*.

Those who *despise* an action *look down* on it.

An *inspector looks* carefully *into* the circumstances of a crime.

A composition with *perspicuity* is easily *seen through*, or understood.

Vocabulary Check

For each sentence, fill each blank with an appropriate word from the list at the right.

1. If you go to the airport _____ a friend, you will watch for him or her carefully.
2. It is useless to _____ on the causes of the argument.
3. A fire of _____ origin must be investigated.
4. A football game is an entertaining event for all the _____.
5. To decide an issue fairly, you should consider all the sides, or _____.

aspects
expecting
spectators
speculate
suspicious

Research Skills

Lesson 33 focuses on getting facts, a part of the first step of the writing process. You first learned about getting facts in Practical Suggestions for Writing, the introductory section in which the writing process is outlined. For gathering materials, you will find suggestions on using the library and Internet. You will also learn to choose reliable resources, take useful notes, and record documentary information to be developed later into citations and a bibliography. In addition, this lesson will show you how to avoid plagiarism and how to write a summary.

33a Using the Library

As you begin your research, look carefully at how long your paper should be, and consider whether you need to limit your topic. Civil rights, for example, is not a subject for a three-page research paper but for a book. You would need to narrow your topic, perhaps to just one right, for example, the right to free expression. As you continue to do research, you may decide that you need to narrow it even further. Keep narrowing your topic until you are confident that you can discuss it adequately in the amount of space you are allowed.

Much of the material that you will need to write a research paper can be found at your college library or at a local library. Libraries like these usually have access to other libraries, so if the item you need is not available, it can often be ordered for you. Learn to use the following library resources:

Library Catalogs

A library catalog lists all the books, magazines, newspapers, journals, CDs, DVDs, and other items the library owns. It does not list individual magazine or newspaper articles. Most library catalogues are computerized. You can search for items by title or author. You can also do a subject search (*civil rights*). Many library catalogs can be accessed on the Internet.

Reference Books

Reference books include dictionaries, encyclopedias, indexes to periodicals (magazines and newspapers), and many other resources. They provide general background articles, definitions, facts, and other information on a variety of subjects. Here is a list of some reference works with which you should be familiar:

Dictionaries

American Heritage Dictionary of the English Language
American Heritage Dictionary: Third Edition (Mass Market Paper)
Merriam-Webster's Collegiate Dictionary, 10th Edition

Encyclopedias

Encyclopedia Americana	General articles on many subjects.
Encyclopedia Britannica	General articles on many subjects.
Encyclopedia of Associations	Nonprofit associations worldwide.
Benet's Reader's Encyclopedia	Subjects having to do with literature.
Encyclopedia of the World's Nations	Data on every nation in the world.

Biographies

Dictionary of American Biography	Comprehensive index.
Oxford Dictionary of National Biography	British; 4th century A.D.–2000.
Who's Who in America	Updated yearly.

Miscellaneous Works

Reader's Guide to Periodical Literature	Index of magazine articles from 1901 to present.
Roget's Thesaurus	Dictionary of synonyms.
The World Factbook	Brief data for every nation.

Online Databases

Many libraries subscribe to online databases. These databases give you access to thousands of magazine, newspaper, and journal articles far beyond the library's holdings. Some are general. Others focus on particular subject areas such as business and finance, music, medicine, and science. Online databases may include some of the reference books listed above, such as *Encyclopedia Britannica*.

33b Using the Internet

With the sheer size of the Internet, it is sometimes difficult to know where to start in order to find good, reliable resources for a paper. Your school or library Web site may have a directory of Web sites for different topics assembled by instructors or librarians. Online resources such as the Internet Public Library (http://www.ipl.org) also provide such directories. The following Web sites can serve as good starting points for research:

Search Engines

These sites include three standard search engines and one metasearch engine, MetaCrawler (it searches several engines at once).

Galaxy	http://www.galaxy.com
Google	http://www.google.com
HotBot	http://www.hotbot.com
MetaCrawler	http://www.metacrawler.com

General References

These sites provide one-stop access to a number of useful resources, such as dictionaries, encyclopedias, almanacs, atlases, calculators, and links to factual information on many subjects.

Information Please	http://www.infoplease.com
Microsoft® Encarta® multimedia encyclopedia	http://encarta.msn.com
Virtual Reference Desk	http://www.refdesk.com

Dictionaries

These sites include two standard dictionaries and OneLook, which searches hundreds of dictionaries simultaneously.

Merriam-Webster Online	http://www.m-w.com
Microsoft® Encarta® multimedia encyclopedia	http://encarta.msn.com, choose Dictionary
OneLook	http://www.onelook.com

Miscellaneous

World Factbook	http://www.cia.gov/cia/ publications/factbook
Literary Criticism	http://www.ipl.org/div/litcrit
Research & Writing	http://www.ipl.org/div/aplus
Merriam-Webster Thesaurus	http://www.m-w.com
Online Conversion	http://www.onlineconversion.com

33c Weighing Authorities

How can you judge whether a book, Web site, or other resource that you are considering using for your paper is reliable? Although it is impossible to give rules that apply in every instance, these suggestions may help you:

In science and other subjects in which knowledge continues to increase, recent material is better than older material. Remember, however, that what matters is when a work was written or last revised by the author rather than the date of the last reprinting. For Web pages, look for the date that the page was created or last updated.

Try to find out something about the author. What are the author's qualifications? Is he or she an authority in the field? Often you can find the answers to these questions in *Who's Who, Who's Who in America,* and other biographical dictionaries.

It is the work itself, however, that should influence you most. If you are considering a book, for example, look at the title page and preface, and try to determine its purpose. Does it seem to seek the truth about something? Do you think the author is attempting to make a reputation or present just one point of view?

Ask similar questions about every resource, including magazine articles and information you find on the Internet. Remember the three questions for critical thinking on page 4. Even if you ask only "Is it possible I could be wrong—or right—about this?" you will have taken a giant step in weighing authorities.

33d Taking Notes

Taking notes will help you gather information and even organize your thoughts. Whatever method you choose for taking notes, you need to follow several guidelines to make sure that your notes are clear, complete, and correct.

- If you use 4 × 6 cards, write neatly and leave space between your ideas. Quote the author's exact words, or summarize them in your own words.
- If you use a laptop computer, identify the source of each note with a complete citation.
- If you use a copy machine, write down details about the source directly on the photocopy.
- When possible, space notes widely to leave room for corrections or additions. Underline important words and phrases.

33e Writing a Summary

A summary is a brief description of a piece of writing that contains just the essential ideas and facts. The ability to write a clear, complete summary is of value in many situations. Summarizing a book or an article can help you decide whether to use it in your paper. Summarizing lecture notes can help you study. A summary at the end of a paper or after an oral presentation reminds the audience of your main points. In business reports and articles in professional journals, a summary helps people decide what to read.

Summaries can be as short as a single sentence or as long as several pages. For college papers and short business reports, they are often a paragraph. In summarizing, follow these guidelines:

1. Read carefully and thoughtfully to find the main idea.

2. Reread for supporting or secondary ideas.

3. Write your summary—substituting when possible a word for a phrase or clause and a phrase for a clause or sentence. Omit everything but essential ideas and facts.

4. Edit and proofread your summary.

33f Citing Your Sources

When you summarize the work of another writer, when you put that person's words or ideas into your own words, or when you quote any portion—however brief—of someone's writing, you need to cite your source. In Lesson 35, you will learn how to set up this information in a paper using footnotes or another method of citation. For now, however, you need to know what information you should record from a source:

- Author's full name
- Title of the book, article, Web site, or other source. For articles, record the title of the article itself and of the source it came from, such as a magazine, newspaper, or journal.
- Place and date of publication
- Page number(s)

33g Being Original—Avoiding Plagiarism

At each stage of the writing process, guard against using someone else's words or ideas as your own. To do so brings the grave charge of plagiarism. What should you do?

- When possible, use your own words and ideas. Think about what an author says, and draw your own conclusions from it.
- Follow the guidelines in 33f on what kind of information needs to be documented.
- When you summarize or put an author's ideas in your own words, signal this clearly with expressions like "According to William Manchester" or "Manchester believes."
- Set up direct quotations properly, quote exactly, and credit the source with a footnote or another method of citation.

Plagiarism from the Internet is a serious problem. Sometimes students fail to understand that text and graphics on the Internet, like text from a book or magazine, must never be used without proper credit. You cannot simply copy and paste material from the Internet into a paper.

When you take information from the Internet to serve as a source for a paper, mark it clearly right away so that you will know it is source material and not your own words. It should go without saying that you should never use papers from free or pay term paper services. Your work must always be your own.

Get the Facts

1. Find the following information. At the end of each answer, list the book or Internet source you consulted.

Apply It !

   a. Find the definition of the word *putative* and two synonyms for it.
   b. Find an authoritative biography of Thomas Jefferson, Langston Hughes, Ray Charles, or Jane Goodall. Write a paragraph explaining why you think the biography is authoritative.
   c. Find a general encyclopedia article about NAFTA. Write a paragraph summarizing the article.
   d. Find some facts about the people, government, and economy of Belarus.
   e. Find a magazine article by John McPhee.
   f. Convert 28 ounces to grams.
   g. List five astronomical societies in the United States.
   h. Who wrote *Up from Slavery* and when was it published?
   i. Who is the Secretary of State in your state? What are his or her party, career, and salary?
   j. Where was Achilles vulnerable, and why? What killed him?
   k. How many patents for inventions did Thomas Edison hold?
   l. What are the benefits of the mineral chromium?

2. Research one of the following topics. Find at least three authoritative resources that you could use to write a three- to five-page paper. Save your research for the next lesson.

   • A famous person
   • A profile of your career field: required education and skills, jobs, career paths, and salaries
   • A major city anywhere in the world
   • A nonfiction book or article that you are interested in reviewing

IMPROVE YOUR VOCABULARY
Roots and Prefixes

TEND, TENT, TENS: stretch, strain

Prefixes

    ad (*at*): to, at, toward
    e, ex: out
    ob: before

Examples

You *attend* when you *stretch* or apply your mind *toward* what is being said.

People without money are in *attenuated* circumstances because their resources are *stretched* thin.

To *extend* one's arm is to *stretch* it *out*.

Ostentation is unnecessary display, showing off or *stretching* one's success before others.

A *tent* is a temporary shelter made from fabric *stretched* over poles.

Vocabulary Check

For each sentence, fill each blank with an appropriate word from the list at the right.

1. The _____ of a flood is the area over which it stretches.
2. A _____ is a stretching or moving in the direction of something.
3. In an athletic _____ , the competitors strain for a victory.
4. The more a rope is stretched, the greater the _____ or strain.
5. A _____ situation is one in which nerves are overstretched.

contest
extent
tendency
tense
tension

Composition

This lesson covers what you will need to know about composition.

34a Unity. A oneness achieved by including the necessary facts and eliminating the unnecessary ones.

34b Coherence. A clear presentation that results from the arrangement of topics in an easy-to-follow way.

34c Emphasis. The stressing of certain parts to make them stand out from the rest; in addition, giving ideas an amount of space in proportion to their importance.

34d The essay. A short composition on any subject.

The same guidelines that apply to the sentence and paragraph apply to all forms of composition. What is composition? Whenever you write—a book report, a letter, an essay, an answer to a question on an examination, or an e-mail—you are *composing*. These guidelines therefore apply to everything you write.

The principle of Unity deals with the selection of material, the principle of Coherence deals with the arrangement of material, and the principle of Emphasis has to do with the arrangement of material with a view to indicating its importance.

34a Unity

The first thing you need to realize when you start to write is that it is necessary not only to make each paragraph a unit but also to make all the paragraphs together constitute a whole. This is accomplished by the separation of ideas to be discussed in different paragraphs and the selection of material.

Suggestions

Include anything essential to the main idea of your composition. Keep your purpose in mind as you write, and think about whom you are writing for. When you finish a section, read it over and ask yourself, have I told the reader everything he or she needs to know about this? Make sure you include enough information for your reader to understand your subject.

Eliminate anything that does not contribute to the main subject. Remember that the principle of Unity is a practical one and needs to be constantly applied. Many facts belong; others do not. Leave out anything that does not help to develop or support the main idea of your composition.

34b Coherence

A composition with coherence is clear and easy to understand. Thoughts flow smoothly, held together in a logical order and linked with transitional expressions. For your writing to have coherence, you must arrange your thoughts in such a way that your reader can follow your train of thought from beginning to end.

Suggestions

Arrange your paragraphs in a logical order. Each kind of composition has its characteristic chain of thought. In narration, you would introduce ideas in the order of time; in description, in the order of position; and in exposition or argument, in the order of similarity, contrast, and the like. (See examples of the four kinds of paragraphs in Lesson 32.)

If possible, list at the outset what points you plan to discuss. One way of showing a reader how your writing is organized is to list at the outset the points you will talk about and then, as each comes up in turn, to refer to that list. A good example of this method is seen in the following sentence, which begins a theme entitled "What Our Town Needs Most":

> The greatest needs of our town are a new high school, a police station, and a larger athletic field.

The three succeeding paragraphs, accordingly, deal with these needs in turn and begin as follows:

A new high school is greatly needed.
A new police station has long been desired.
The third need that we are concerned with is a larger athletic field.

When you follow this method, first outlining your plan and then showing that you are adhering to it, you make it easy for the reader to understand and follow the course of your theme.

Use transitions to connect ideas. As you move from one paragraph to another, you must indicate to the reader how what you have just written is related to what comes next. Transitions can include the words and phrases you learned about in Lesson 32, such as *furthermore*, *in addition*, and *accordingly*. But they can also include whole sentences that help to link the current paragraph to the previous one. Note how the underscored words and sentences in the second paragraph connect to those in the first and help the reader follow the discussion:

Credit cards are a fact of college life. According to a <u>recent study</u>, some 83 percent of undergraduates have at least one. <u>These students are quick to point to the advantages of having a credit card while in school</u>. Credit cards, they tell you, help them manage their living expenses, establish a good credit record, pay for travel, and handle emergencies.

<u>Yet, for college students, credit cards have disadvantages as well.</u> <u>The same study</u> found that in four years of college, students who hold credit cards triple the number of cards they hold—and double what they owe. Furthermore, by the time they graduate, nearly a third of these students have racked up credit card debts of $3,000 to $7,000.

34c Emphasis

As you have learned, emphasis is the principle in which certain parts are stressed so that they stand out from the rest. That is, the ideas that you wish to impress most strongly on the reader should be placed in those parts of the composition most likely to be seen. Another way of using emphasis effectively is to give ideas an amount of space in proportion to their importance.

Suggestions

Put important ideas in prominent positions. As in the sentence and the paragraph, Emphasis in the composition demands that the most important ideas be placed at the beginning and end.

First sentences give readers their first impressions. They introduce the topic and set the tone for what will follow. Think carefully, therefore, about how you will begin your composition. Here are some suggestions:

- List at the outset what points you plan to discuss.
- State the purpose of your composition.
- Tell what led you to write it.
- Relate an interesting story.
- Ask one or more appropriate questions.

The ending is the most emphatic position. This part should give an impression of completeness to your writing and should leave the reader with something to remember. The most effective conclusion is often a summary of your most important points. The following example is from a theme on "My First Business Experience":

> As I look back on that experience, I cannot see that it deepened my appreciation of the value of money, nor do I regret that fact. I enjoyed it, and in the end, I think that my venture was a success.

Give each idea an amount of space proportionate to its importance. Plan your work so that each idea will have an amount of space proportionate to its importance. The following example shows how failing to plan can result in poor proportion. In a theme entitled "The Needs of Our College," the author devotes three paragraphs to discussing the college's needs:

> What our college needs most is a good library.
> (Begins a paragraph of fifty words.)

> Next among our needs is, I believe, a physical fitness center.
> (Begins a paragraph of fifty words.)

> The last need, and also the least important, is a better system of marking.
> (Begins a paragraph of one hundred words.)

If the third need is the least important, it should not have one-half the theme given to it. Fifty or sixty words at most is all that it should receive. As it is now, the reader has an abundance of information on the least important need and half as much on the two more important ones.

34d The Essay

The essay is a short composition on any subject. There are many kinds of essays. Some, for example, describe. Others compare one thing to another. Some try to persuade the reader. A book review is a variety of an essay.

A traditional essay consists of five paragraphs: the introduction (one paragraph) the body (three paragraphs), and the conclusion (one paragraph). Essays may be longer or shorter than five paragraphs depending on the topic and the requirements of the assignment.

The outline. Make an outline before starting your essay. It will save time, help you to organize your work, and show where you may need to add or take away material before you begin writing. You will find no exercise of more value than that of making an outline.

The introduction. A good introduction will tell your readers what to expect in the body of the essay and will make them want to keep reading. For this part, you might include a **thesis statement,** a sentence containing the main idea of your essay. Here is an example of an introductory paragraph:

> In 1747, a Scottish physician named James Lind revolutionized the treatment of scurvy. In a famous experiment, Lind showed that scurvy, a disease that had killed millions of people throughout history, could be cured simply by consuming oranges and lemons. This idea was slow to take hold—one reason being that ship captains and owners found carrying these fruits expensive and troublesome.

The body. The body is the central part of your essay—the place where you turn the ideas you have planned to write about into effective paragraphs that develop and support your main idea. By rereading the introductory paragraph, you can guess which points would be developed in the body of this essay:

- A description of scurvy and the toll it took
- Information on the study Lind made
- A discussion of why Lind's findings were not acted on immediately

The conclusion. A good conclusion will summarize the information in the body of the essay and make readers believe they have read something worthwhile and informative. Here is an example of a concluding paragraph:

James Lind prevented a great deal of suffering and saved many lives by establishing the superiority of citrus fruits over other remedies for scurvy. Yet, despite the fact that the disease was killing more sailors than enemy action, it took more than forty years for the British Royal Navy to require ships to carry citrus fruit. The difficulties that arose in getting this simple remedy adopted are an example of obstacles still encountered by scientists and physicians today.

Apply It!

Write an Essay

In this activity, draft a three- to five-page essay on the topic you chose in the last lesson's Apply It! activity. Save your work for Lesson 35.

- **A famous person.** Write a short biography of the person you selected. Discuss his or her childhood, education, family, life as an adult, work, and significant accomplishments.

- **A profile of your career field.** Explain the educational background and skills required to enter your career field. Sketch some career paths that interest you. Note salaries for several jobs as well as working conditions and job outlook.

- **A major city anywhere in the world.** Describe the city you chose. Explain where it is located, when it was founded, why it is important, what kinds of buildings it has, and any other interesting facts about it.

- **A book.** Review a work of nonfiction, either a book or an article. Include some or all of these points:

  1. **Introduction.** Tell something about the author. Was the author qualified to write the book or article?
  2. **A brief outline of what the author was trying to say.** Can you explain the point or points the author was trying to make?
  3. **Criticism of the author's statements.** Do you agree with the author? Would this information be helpful to others?
  4. **Criticism of the author's style.** Is the author clear and concise? Are the words simple and specific? Are there any unnecessary technical expressions? Are the sentences clear, concise, and varied?
  5. **The reason the article or book was written.** Was there a need for information on this subject? Did the author write it to present needed information or to entertain? Did you find it worthwhile to read?

Note: Use brief quotations to illustrate the author's style or any special point.

IMPROVE YOUR VOCABULARY
Roots and Prefixes

VERT: turn

Prefixes

> *ad*: to, at
> *contra, contro*: against
> *re*: again, back

Examples

> *Adversity* is trouble or misfortune, events that have *turned* against you.
>
> *Advertisers turn* the mind or attention of buyers to their wares.
>
> To *avert* is to *turn* away from: to attempt to ward off or prevent.
>
> A *controversy* is a dispute in which all sides have *turned against* each other.
>
> *Vertigo* is dizziness, a *turning* or whirling sensation.

Vocabulary Check

For each sentence, fill each blank with an appropriate word from the list at the right.

1. _____ humor criticizes, or tends to turn over, the conventions of society.
2. When dividing fractions, you _____ the second one (turn it upside down) and multiply.
3. To _____ a stream is to change its course, or turn it in another direction.
4. To _____ a slide into a Web page is to turn one thing into another.
5. To _____ direction is to turn around and go the opposite way.

convert
divert
invert
reverse
subversive

Lesson 35

The Final Steps

This lesson covers the final steps to writing effectively.

35a   **Revise.**

35b   **Prepare your finished copy.**

In Practical Suggestions for Writing, you learned about the five steps of the writing process. In Lesson 35, you will learn more about Step 4, Revise. You remember that the secret of success in writing effectively lies in revision, the careful improvement of your work. You will also learn more about Step 5, Prepare Your Finished Copy. You will learn a simple method of formatting papers, with steps and tips for proof-reading.

35a Revise

Set aside what you have written, preferably for a day or more, but at least for several hours. Then read it aloud slowly, or have someone else read it. The revision checklist on the following page is based on the great principles of Unity, Coherence, and Emphasis. Use it as a guide for improving your work.

Become acquainted with the features of your word processing software that can help you in revision. Use cut, copy, and paste to rearrange material. Use find and replace to locate and correct text. Use bullets and numbers to organize lists. And use the thesaurus when you need to vary your wording or find just the right word.

The Composition

- If you have included a thesis statement, does it state your main idea clearly?
- Does each paragraph support your main idea?
- Have you arranged your paragraphs in a logical order?
- Do you have a strong introduction and conclusion?

The Paragraph

- Does each paragraph have a topic sentence? If not, can you summarize the paragraph in a single sentence?
- For each paragraph, have you supplied necessary facts and eliminated unnecessary ones?
- Have you used appropriate transitions to connect ideas?
- Have you placed important sentences at the beginnings and endings of paragraphs?

The Sentence

- Is every sentence clear and logical?
- Can you make your sentences more concise? Can you change a clause to a phrase? A clause to an appositive? A phrase to a word? Have you cut excess wordage?
- Can you make a verb active rather than passive?
- Do your sentences show variety?
- Have you eliminated sentences with the same thought unless for emphasis?

Words

- Can you replace a pretentious word with a simple one?
- Can you substitute a specific word for a general one?
- Have you eliminated outdated expressions?

35b Prepare Your Finished Copy

For many writing assignments in college and at work, you will be given a format that you should follow. Businesses, for example, usually have set formats for letters and memos. In other cases, you will need to determine a format on your own. This section provides a simple method of formatting essays and other college papers.

A title page should be centered vertically so that there is the same amount of space at the top as at the bottom. Your word processing software will center the page for you. In Microsoft® Word, choose Page Setup from the File menu; choose the Layout tab; and choose Center from Vertical alignment. A sample title page is shown in Figure 35-1.

Figure 35-1

Title Page

- Center each line.
- Center the page vertically (your word processor has a feature for this).
- Leave about eight lines between parts.

COLLEGE SPORTS AND MONEY

↓ 8

by
Lynn C. Rogers

↓ 8

Professor Malcolm Potter
English Composition II

↓ 8

March 15, 200_

Body

The body of a paper is double-spaced and uses the standard margin settings of your word processor. Pages are numbered at the top right. The title page is not included in the page numbering.

To set page numbers in Microsoft® Word, choose Page Numbers from the Insert menu. Choose "Top of page (header)." Do not select the box that says "Show number on first page." To get the pages to number properly, you will need to create your paper as a separate document from your title page. A sample first page from the body of a paper is shown in Figure 35-2.

Figure 35-2

- Use standard margin settings.
- Do not put a page number on the first page.

2"

FORMAT FOR COLLEGE PAPERS

Correct formatting makes college papers more attractive and readable. This report gives you simple formatting guidelines for essays and other college papers.

General Setup

You do not need to change the margins of your word processing software for a college paper. The standard margin settings are fine. The first page should start about two inches from the top. Press Enter a few times to get to about two inches, and then begin keying. In many word processors, you can tell how far down you are from the status bar at the bottom of the page.

Use Times Roman in the 12-point font size for the body of your paper. You can make the title a little bigger. Use double spacing, except for long quotations, numbered or bulleted items, and references.

Quotations

Quotations are formatted in one of two ways depending on how long they are. Quotations up to three lines long appear in the paragraph in quotation marks. For example, William Strunk, Jr., wrote, "Revision is part of writing. Few writers are so expert that they can produce what they are after on the first try" (1972, 64). Longer quotations are single-spaced and indented from the left margin:

> Quotations are effective in research papers when used selectively. Quote only words, phrases, lines, and passages that are particularly interesting, vivid, or apt, and keep all quotations as brief as possible. Overquotation can bore your readers and might lead them to conclude that you are neither an original thinker nor a skillful writer. (Gibaldi, 1995, 72)

The references page should be the last page of your paper. Insert a manual page break at the end of your paper to start a new page for the references.

In Figure 35-3, note that the second and following lines of each reference are indented. This is called a **hanging indent**. Your word processor has a hanging indent feature. In Microsoft® Word, choose Paragraph from the Format menu, and choose Hanging from Special.

Figure 35-3

References.

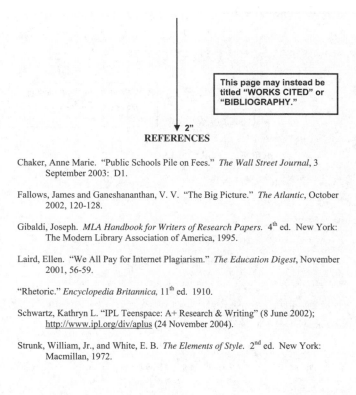

This page may instead be titled "WORKS CITED" or "BIBLIOGRAPHY."

↓ 2"

REFERENCES

Chaker, Anne Marie. "Public Schools Pile on Fees." *The Wall Street Journal*, 3 September 2003: D1.

Fallows, James and Ganeshananthan, V. V. "The Big Picture." *The Atlantic*, October 2002, 120-128.

Gibaldi, Joseph. *MLA Handbook for Writers of Research Papers.* 4th ed. New York: The Modern Library Association of America, 1995.

Laird, Ellen. "We All Pay for Internet Plagiarism." *The Education Digest*, November 2001, 56-59.

"Rhetoric." *Encyclopedia Britannica,* 11th ed. 1910.

Schwartz, Kathryn L. "IPL Teenspace: A+ Research & Writing" (8 June 2002); http://www.ipl.org/div/aplus (24 November 2004).

Strunk, William, Jr., and White, E. B. *The Elements of Style.* 2nd ed. New York: Macmillan, 1972.

Formatting References

There are many ways of formatting the references that you use in a paper, but they all fall into three main types: internal citations, footnotes, and endnotes.

With internal citations, you put a short citation following the material you wish to reference in parentheses and a list of all the references you have used for your paper at the end. Internal citations are shown in Figures 35-2 and 35-3.

For footnotes and endnotes, you place a superscript number[1] in your paper and a corresponding number and footnote at the bottom of the page (footnotes) or at the end of your paper (endnotes). A footnote or endnote looks like this:

[1]Mark Sullivan, *Our Times: The United States 1900–1925* (New York: Charles Scribner's Sons, 1927), p. 488.

Word processors have a special feature that creates footnotes and endnotes for you. In Microsoft® Word, this feature is found in the Insert menu and is called Reference or Footnote, depending on the version you are using.

College instructors most often ask their students to use MLA (Modern Language Association) style and APA (American Psychological Association) style. Both methods use internal citations, though in a slightly different format than that shown in Figures 35-2 and 35-3. Many resources are available to show you how to format citations in MLA or APA style:

- *MLA Handbook for Writers of Research Papers* by Joseph Gibaldi is the official MLA handbook. This handbook is available in the reference section of many libraries.
- *Publication Manual* is the title of the APA handbook. It, too, is available in the reference section of many libraries.
- Many Web sites provide guidelines on MLA or APA formatting. To find such a Web site, key "apa style" or "mla style" in a search engine.
- The APA Web site provides guidelines on formatting electronic references such as Web sites at http://www.apastyle.org.

A bibliography is an alphabetized list of the books, articles, Web resources, and other materials that you used in writing your paper. It is sometimes called **References** or **Works Cited**. Figure 35-3 shows some standard bibliographic entries that you may use if your instructor does not recommend a format.

Proofreading

Proofreading is a last check for errors. For papers, proofread after you have revised and formatted your copy. Letters, memos, e-mails, and other documents should be proofread just before sending.

Look for errors in keying, punctuation, spelling, grammar, and formatting. Bigger errors should have been detected and corrected during revision, but be alert for those errors as well. Look especially for the kinds of errors that you know you are prone to make. The following steps will help you to be a good proofreader:

1. If possible, allow some time to pass between revising or preparing a document and proofreading it.
2. Just before proofreading, run the spelling and grammar check features. For e-mail, run the spelling feature.
3. Proofread the document on screen first.
4. Proofread the printed document. Use an envelope or ruler. Move it down line by line so that you will focus on one line at a time.

As you probably know, you cannot depend upon your computer to find all errors. Use the following guidelines therefore to catch any faults:

- Are two sentences written as one? Is a part of a sentence written as a sentence?
- Are there any errors in subject-verb agreement, subject and object forms of pronouns, the incorrect forms of verbs, and the like?
- Are compound sentences, introductory elements, interrupting elements, and words and phrases in a series correctly punctuated?
- Are apostrophes, hyphens, capitalization, and the like correct?
- Are there any spelling errors such as *it's/its*, *to/too*, and *there/their*?

Apply It

Revise and Format an Essay

1. Revise the essay you wrote in Lesson 34. Use the checklist presented earlier in this lesson as a guide in editing your work. Use features of your word processing software such as find, replace, and thesaurus.

2 Format your revised essay using the formatting guidelines presented in this lesson. Use features of your word processing software such as double spacing, font size, and automatic numbering.

3. Proofread your final copy using the steps and guidelines for proofreading given in the preceding section. Make any needed corrections.

IMPROVE YOUR VOCABULARY
A Final Check

Match Prefixes With Definitions

1. _____ a, ab, abs   A. before
2. _____ ad (ac, ap, at)   B. two, twice
3. _____ ante   C. to, at, toward
4. _____ bi   D. from, away
5. _____ circum   E. around, about

6. _____ com, con   A. against, opposite
7. _____ contra, contro   B. with, together
8. _____ de   C. from, down
9. _____ dis   D. out, out of, from
10. _____ e, ex   E. apart, not

11. _____ in (im)   A. among, between
12. _____ inter   B. in, on, into, against, not
13. _____ ob (op)   C. through, by
14. _____ per   D. before
15. _____ pre   E. against, in the way

16. _____ pro   A. for, forth, forward, before
17. _____ re   B. beyond, above, over
18. _____ sub   C. again, back
19. _____ super   D. under, below
20. _____ trans   E. over, beyond, across, through

Match Roots With Definitions

1. _____ cap, cep, cip   A. move, go, yield
2. _____ cede, ceed, cess   B. speak, say
3. _____ dict   C. take, seize, grasp
4. _____ duct, duc   D. do, make
5. _____ fac, fact, fect, fic   E. lead, bring, draw

6. _____ mal   A. look at, see
7. _____ mit, miss   B. turn
8. _____ pend, pond, pen   C. send, let go
9. _____ spect, spic   D. weigh, hang
10. _____ vert   E. bad, evil

APPENDIX A

Consider the Reader

Considering the reader—the "you" attitude—is an important aspect of the writing process. It is a viewpoint that practically guarantees you will write an effective composition or letter since you will want to make your writing as clear as possible in order to save your reader time and energy.

The following questions will help you to have this "you" attitude. In addition, they will help you get along well with others, a key skill desired by employers. Even if you find you already have a good attitude, learn how to put your good intentions into practice by asking yourself these questions and following these guidelines.

1. **Can you be depended on to do what you say you will do?** Do not promise, for example, to go to a school function with a friend, write an article for the school newspaper, or work late unless you are reasonably sure that you can do this. Trying to do what you said you would do is important for this reason: It helps make you a dependable person. When someone reneges on a promise, most of us are not only disappointed in the broken promise but in the person who made the promise.

2. **Do you go out of your way to help others?** If a friend asks for help with a homework assignment or someone asks you to volunteer for a good cause and you can honestly do it, say yes. Being in the habit of helping others when possible is a positive thing. It tells others you care about them—and in the end can result in a benefit to you.

3. **Are you careful not to exaggerate?** When writing a letter of application and a resume, for example, be cautious not to overstate your qualifications; instead, present your abilities honestly and truthfully. Exaggerating your abilities can actually backfire on you. If you are hired for a position and then do not have certain abilities, you could cause yourself great stress—and even possibly lose the position.

4. **Do you resist the temptation to be sarcastic?** Even when a person is truly insufferable, refrain from answering sarcastically. Although sarcasm is never acceptable, criticism and sarcasm are particularly offensive in e-mail.

5. **Do you try to keep from feeling superior to others?** If you are in the capacity of supervising others, you especially need to guard against becoming impatient with their progress. Tolerance of those who are less knowledgeable can be a difficult task. Keep in mind, though, that this principle is considered one of the outstanding qualities of leadership.

6. **Do you always try to control your temper?** If someone deliberately antagonizes you, it is often difficult to refrain from becoming angry. Always keep in mind that "A soft answer turns away wrath, but a harsh word stirs up anger." Putting your reaction in writing, incidentally, is not only counterproductive but can bring you great distress later.

7. **Can you forgive and forget?** You cannot get along with people if you carry grudges. The other person may be wrong, but in the end it serves no purpose to be unpleasant because of a misunderstanding that occurred months or even years ago. Such a practice could be injurious to your own well being.

8. **Do you avoid asking favors of others and borrowing items?** Such actions place your friends and associates in a compromising position. If they do not really want to comply with your requests, they could find themselves hesitant to deny what you want for fear of offending you.

9. **Are you careful not to gossip?** Even if true, malicious gossip can mar a person's good name and ultimately reflect back on your reputation. Making unsubstantiated negative comments can cause even greater difficulty, including lawsuits for libel.

10. **Do you refrain from telling people they are wrong?** It's been suggested that you try to understand why people act as they do and then ask yourself how you would feel if you were in their place. If it is necessary to point out another's errors, however, a good suggestion is first to mention your own mistakes.

11. **Are you fair?** As explained in Practical Suggestions for Writing, unfairness is usually the result of selfishness, and there are many opportunities to be honest and fair. In business, fairness plays an important part in letters intended to adjust differences. But even in matters such as who pays for lunch, making sure you do not take advantage of others is not only sensible but fair.

12. **Are you tactful?** Tact, the perception of the right thing to say without offending others, summarizes all the other qualities. As explained in Practical Suggestions for Writing, the Golden Rule—do unto others as you would have them do unto you—is perhaps the best definition of this great skill.

APPENDIX B

Apply It! Solutions

Part 1

Lesson 1—The Parts of Speech
Answers. 1. noun 2. verb 3. noun 4. preposition 5. adjective 6. noun 7. noun 8. verb 9. adjective 10. noun 11. noun 12. verb 13. adjective 14. noun

Lesson 2—Stage One of the Sentence
Answers. 1. day/was 2. opportunities/are offered 3. Neither/has been ordered 4. company/has purchased 5. They/smiled, continued 6. container/cooled, solidified 7. Many/were sold 8. president/did report 9. amount/was 10. letters, gifts/ pour 11. [You]/sound 12. manager/is 13. ticket/is stamped; it/is 14. They/practiced, they/had 15. charges/are; tax/is required

Lesson 3—Stage Two of the Sentence
Answers. 1. managers/are/professionals 2. students/can learn/lessons 3. pronunciation/is/incorrect 4. workers/received/bonus 5. I/do understand/appraisal 6. bookkeeper/found/errors 7. manager/drew/plan 8. we/added/room 9. She/presented/gift 10. fire/warmed/hands 11. scout/followed/parade 12. leaves/dropped 13. They/walked 14. He/manages/business 15. game/was/exciting

Lesson 4—Stage Three of the Sentence
Answers. 1. students/left 2. she/will correct/it 3. I/will be 4. person/was/associate 5. Riding a bicycle/can be/strenuous 6. That she is a famous actress/is known 7. Ms. Tucker/is/founder 8. half/will disappear 9. account/will be cancelled 10. We/listened 11. People/look/facts 12. Roger/brought/books 13. I/will secure/loan 14. they/attended/meetings 15. telegram/arrived

Part 2

Lesson 5—Writing for Information
Note: Correct verbs are underlined and in bold type.

In writing for information, you need to be clear in your mind as to exactly what it is you want to know. After you decide this, arrange your letter to make it easy for your reader to find the items you are requesting. If a variety of points **is** being covered, tabulation is often useful.

Requests for routine information should be as brief as possible—consistent with courtesy and clarity. In writing for a pamphlet, using a letterhead and keeping your request to the essentials can be of great help. The quality of stationery and envelopes **is** important to show that you are in business or have financial responsibility.

Lesson 6—Increasing Vocabulary
Note: Correct verbs are underlined and in bold type. A C indicates that the sentence is correct.
1. The number of words in the English language is over 600,000. C
2. This news, useful for success in life, **appears** in many articles.
3. *Four Ways to Increase Your Vocabulary* is a valuable reference. C
4. A number of students **were** using crossword puzzles to increase vocabulary.
5. Twenty dollars, in fact, is the correct price for the speed-reading course. C
6. Penny is one of those students who find the vocabulary practice helpful. C
7. Most of the students also find drill and practice effective. C
8. The number of people seeking improvement is increasing. C

9. Some of the advice includes talking to well-informed people and reading good books and magazines. C
10. Most of it involves using the dictionary and finding new words. C
11. Some of the new telecommunications terms have been accepted by the general public. C
12. A thesaurus is one of the most useful references that **are** required for composition classes.

Lesson 7—On Campus

Note: Correct pronouns are underlined and in bold type.

1. The English class is traveling to Russia with Regina and **me**.
2. Ellen, Eugene, and **I** were appointed tutors.
3. The loud explosion did not frighten my friend and **me**.
4. No one signed up for the Saturday class except Paul and **me**.
5. June and **I** arrived at the dormitory at the same time.
6. David sent my friend and **me** two tickets to the homecoming game.
7. The testing schedule was sent to my classmates and **me**.
8. The debating club sent Grace and **me** a book.
9. The lecturer gave the instructor and **me** a copy of the speech.
10. The librarian and **I** made the decision.
11. The instructor objected to **my** inability to complete the assignments on time.
12. The academic awards went to Marilyn and **me**.
13. Few students can keyboard as accurately as **I**.
14. Do you approve of **my** representing the college at the upcoming debate?
15. Neither Craig nor **I** was able to eliminate the computer virus.

Lesson 8—Lying on a Cloud

Note: Correct verbs are underlined and in bold type.

June White was just looking to buy a new headboard for her bed when she strolled into a store near her home in White Plains, New York. She was there with her husband and children, she said, when they started trying out mattresses just for the fun of it. "My husband **lay** down on one of them and just said to the salesperson, 'I want this bed,'" she recalls, laughing. "When I lay on it, I couldn't get up. It was so nice, like lying on a cloud."

They bought it that day. They did not know that they had joined one of the fastest-growing home trends—foam. Several years ago, all the mattresses were made with a framework of metal innersprings surrounded by a layer of foam. Today, more mattresses are made entirely of foam. Such mattresses are not cheap, most costing at least $1,000. That is why June whispered that she wished that she **were** wealthy.

Lesson 9—Patience

Note: Correct adjectives and adverbs are underlined and in bold type.

The researchers found an article on the virtue of patience. **This** kind of document is not usually **really** clear or well written, but this one is the **better** of the two found previously. It reads, "Patience comforts the poor and moderates the rich; it makes us humble in prosperity, cheerful in adversity, and unmoved by calumny."

The researchers concluded that patience, which means the capacity for calm or endurance, is the **best** of the three character traits they investigated.

Lesson 10—Memo on Prepositions

Note: Correct words are underlined and in bold type.

1. In the future, try **to** express yourself more clearly.
2. Hunter dived **into** the water from the pier.
3. The committee differed **with** me about the plans.
4. Destiny's standards of living are different **from** yours.
5. The manager has agreed **to** my proposition.
6. The work should be divided **among** the three consultants.
7. The vice president said the employees should **have** attended the meeting.
8. Please keep **off** the grass.
9. The workers are angry **with** the sales manager.
10. This workstation is different **from** that workstation.

Lesson 11—Letter of Application

Note: Correct words are underlined and in bold type.

In response to your recent *Wall Street Journal* advertisement, I would appreciate **your** considering me an applicant for Developmental Editor. As I will explain, I believe I meet your requirements for this position.

On my own, I have assisted the Board of Trustees in **its** effort to provide a program in which there **is** a variety of positions. Every one of the employees **has** found me to be a person who never **lies** down on the job. Recently my supervisor praised my associate and **me** for our writing ability. She felt **bad** that the others did not recommend us.

Part 3

Lesson 12—The Power of Persuasion

Note: The 8 commas to be added are underlined and in bold type.

Many sales letters fail because they lack the important element of persuasion. Suppose**,** for example**,** that in your letter you gain the attention and interest of your reader, explain the benefits of your product, and prove its real merit. If you bring your remarks abruptly to a close and sign your name, you will probably get some orders. Suppose, however, that instead you show your reader how your product will be of practical value.

Perhaps your readers have never thought of the matter in just that way. Your letter persuades them that your product will put dollars and cents into their pocket. Yes, they are made to see the profit rather than the expense.

Lesson 13—Clearness in Business Writing
Note: The 9 commas to be added are underlined and in bold type.

Business writing needs to be extraordinarily clear. For this reason, the average paragraph should be short—much less than one hundred words and no more than four or five sentences. In business, in fact, even single-sentence paragraphs are sometimes acceptable and even effective. (A long series of two-sentence or so paragraphs, on the other hand, should be avoided since such a monotonous arrangement may distract the reader.)

In order for a paragraph to be clear, the sentences must be in logical order. In addition, words such as however, moreover, and consequently should be used to help the flow of sentences.

Lesson 14—Postponement
Note: The 2 commas and 2 semicolons to be added are underlined and in bold type.

Postponement is a common fault. If you want to fail, try putting off until tomorrow what you can just as well do today. If you want to succeed, on the other hand, consider the value of time. There is an inexhaustible market for it. Whenever you purchase an article of value, you are buying mostly time. Manufacturers take several hundred dollars worth of materials; then they turn them into expensive machines. Watchmakers buy ten dollars' worth of steel; later they turn them into fine springs worth thousands of dollars. Your success depends not only on the kind of time you have to sell but on what you do with the time you have. Do not procrastinate. The road to success is paved with the good intentions of people who do not postpone anything.

Lesson 15—Brevity is Best
Note: The 3 commas and 3 semicolons to be added are underlined and in bold type.

When you write a business letter, you should remember that the person addressed cares only for what we have to say and not for ourselves; this is exactly the reverse of a friendly letter. This is why the chief virtue of a business letter is brevity.

Those who read it want to know what we have to say about our business as quickly as possible; they want to be able to act on it if it is related in any way to their own business and lose no time.

The Anglo Saxon *bisig* is the word from which are derived both business and busy; a businessperson is supposed to be a busy person. Businesspersons, therefore, are too busy to read rambling letters where the message is neither clearly stated nor properly formatted.

Lesson 16—Courtesy Counts
Note: The 6 commas and 1 semicolon to be added are underlined and in bold type.

It is important that you be courteous since discourtesy injures personal relations. Try to be sincere and direct; also, do not attempt to get even with a person who has been discourteous to you. Remember that what may sound all right when spoken may be interpreted entirely differently by your reader. For example, the following sentence might not have been written discourteously:

We have already explained to you the manner in which your orders are handled by us.

If this sentence, however, is read aloud in an angry tone, the effect is entirely changed. Since discourtesy injures business relations, it is important that you be courteous.

Lesson 17—Punctuation Pitfalls
Note: The marks of punctuation to be added are underlined and in bold type.

In your writing, do you ever leave out a question mark or an exclamation point? Pity the poor writers who do so habitually! Are they likely to do well in composition? Never! The period is another mark of which we need to say something. No one with a college—or even high school—education should get into the careless habit of putting commas where periods belong.

1. Three states gave the railroad its name. It was one of the longest and best systems in the country.
2. We spent several years in Italy. It is called the land of laughter and flowers.
3. Mr. Barlow was born in a small Iowa village, and he is now the president of a large telecommunications company. Correct
4. The house had stood empty for seven years. The former owners had moved to another state.

5. The road is overshadowed by giant trees**. T**hey have been growing there for hundreds of years.
6. Despite the severity of the weather, the students came that great distance. Correct
7. We had not driven far when we had a flat tire**. T**his was caused by a nail that we picked up somewhere along the highway.
8. Dr. O'Brien is an instructor at the college**. S**he is also the faculty adviser for the student newspaper.

Lesson 18—The Wisdom of Proverbs

Note: The apostrophes to be added are underlined and in bold type.

1. Another person**'**s burden is always light.
2. An idle brain is the devil**'**s workshop.
3. Another**'**s misfortune does not cure my pain.
4. It is a silly goose that comes to a fox**'**s sermon.
5. Industry is fortune**'**s right hand, and frugality her left.
6. Repentance is the heart**'**s medicine.
7. Kind words heal friendship**'**s wounds.
8. The noblest task is to command one's self.
9. A prudent haste is wisdom**'**s leisure.
10. Order is heaven**'**s first law.
11. Nobody**'**s sweetheart is ugly.
12. A man**'**s home is his castle.
13. The rainbow at night is the shepherd**'**s delight.
14. We carry our neighbors**'** failings in sight; we throw our own over our shoulders.
15. One person**'**s loss is another person's gain.
16. At last, the foxes all meet at the furrier**'**s.
17. A great man**'**s foolish sayings pass for wise ones.
18. Hope is grief**'**s best music.
19. A king**'**s favor is no inheritance.
20. That which is everybody**'**s business is nobody**'**s business.

Lesson 19—A Mark in Distress

Note: The apostrophe corrections are underlined and in bold type.

- Mindy's Sub Shop Open 7 **Days** a Week
- **Women's** and **children's** fashion accessories
- A friend of Mr. **Kelly's**
- A **CEO's** plan for reorganization
- The **Maroneys** have gone to Kansas.
- "Ace Funeral Association Takes Care of **Its** Own" (a slogan)

Lesson 20—Abused Marks of Punctuation

Note: The two single dashes, two sets of dashes, and one set of parentheses to be added are underlined and in bold type.

Now we have to consider the dash**—**a much-abused mark of punctuation. Our thoughts may be running on smoothly when we suddenly digress**—**and unbelievable as it may seem**—**need a mark to indicate the abruptness of the change. You see how our sentences become examples of their own rules concerning other marks of punctuation. Merely remarking that the dash is used generally in enumerations, we will also discuss other instances where there may be doubt as to the best usage**—**dashes in pairs and parentheses.

When we come to discuss parentheses **(**see page 81 for a fuller discussion of this subject**)**, we find that it is sometimes convenient to break into a sentence with an "aside" grammatically independent of the main statement. But sometimes**—**and this sentence is a case in point**—**two dashes are preferable, for they indicate a close connection between the "aside" and the sentence it interrupts.

Lesson 21—Clarifying Colons

Note: The six colons to be added are underlined and in bold type.

The colon has two **uses:** It is used before a formal quotation or enumeration. It is infrequently used between two clauses of a sentence in which the second stands in some sort of apposition with the first. We need not go far for an illustration of the second **use:** the very sentence we write furnishes it.

To make sure you are not confused by the colon, insert a colon where needed in each of the following sentences. If not needed, write a C.

1. Among the qualities everyone should develop are **these:** tact, loyalty, perseverance, and resourcefulness.
2. This is our **advice:** Stay in school and prepare for a career.
3. The seasons of the year are fall, winter, spring, and summer. Correct
4. These are the four courses you **should take:** English, algebra, chemistry, and accounting.
5. The five Great Lakes are Lake Erie, Lake Ontario, Lake Huron, Lake Michigan, and Lake Superior. Correct
6. **Wanted:** experienced accountant.

Lesson 22—A Valuable Mark

Note: The three hyphens to be added are underlined and in bold type.

In addition to contributing to clarity, the use of the hyphen can also contribute to conciseness and emphasis, a **little-known** fact. Study the sentence that follows:

The teachers have gone to a meeting that will last for three hours.

Now if you wish to emphasize *teachers* and *three hours,* this sentence is fine. But if you wish to emphasize *teachers* and *meeting,* you should spotlight the word *meeting* at the end of the sentence—and using the **long-lived** hyphen can make this possible. It can also result in conciseness, a savings of four words.

*The teachers have gone to a **three-hour** meeting.*

Lesson 23—A Sales Message

Note: The quotation mark corrections are underlined and printed in bold type; underlining is used to indicate italics.

Physicians, nurses, and health care professionals—all make a claim for one of the best nutritional magazines on the market today—Nutrition Today. Dr. Jonathon Lopez states, **"**I am a regular reader of this magazine and can honestly say it has no equal.**"**

Nutrition Today can be described as an educational magazine, providing readers with practical information about diet, lifestyle, vitamins, minerals, and other nutrients. Recently, it has published outstanding articles such as **"**Nutrient Profile**"** and **"**Science Update.**"** In the past year, it has also featured such articles as **"**Sports Nutrition: Stocking Your Sports Medicine Chest,**"** **"**The New Vitamin on the Block,**"** and **"**Treatment Plan for the Cold.**"**

Be sure therefore to order Nutrition Today. It is a decision you will never regret. As Dr. Lopez maintains, **"**It has no equal.**"**

Lesson 24—Courtesy Days

Note: The 18 words to be capitalized are in bold type.
Dear Ms. Rains:

As you are one of our preferred customers, we are telling you about **Courtesy Days**, the **August Furniture Sale** that will begin **Thursday, August** 7. We would like our charge customers to have first choice of the great values before they are announced to the public.

We hope therefore that you will join us on one of our three **Courtesy Days—Thursday, Friday**, and **Saturday** of this week—when you may come in and make your selections at the sale prices.

You will find greater variety than usual because we now carry popular brands such as **Timberline** and **Natura World**. You will also find attractive prices this year. We look forward to having you visit us on the most important event of our year—**Courtesy Days**! **Sincerely,**

Lesson 25—Name That Number

Note: The five corrected numbers are printed in bold type.

Dr. Francis asked that we send her 65 copies of our latest brochure. She is conducting **four** workshops and believes that over ten teachers will attend each workshop.

The cost of the brochures is **$225**. There is a **10** percent discount if the bill is paid before April **30**. It is disappointing that only **one half** the class plans to attend. We will be happy to send Dr. Francis the 65 copies.

Part 4

Lesson 26—The Absent-Minded Professor

Note: The four spelling corrections are printed in bold type.

Professor Wilson's **principal** failing was her absent-mindedness. This often led her **to** misplace articles necessary to her teaching. One day as she and another professor were walking on campus, Professor Wilson suddenly stopped, looked perplexed, and said to her friend, "Why, my notes for today's lecture have disappeared. If I don't find those notes, I will disappoint my class."

"What is that in your hand?" her colleague asked.

"Copies of the law review I just picked up at the printing center," she replied. "My notes were in a separate envelope of about the same size."

"Wait a minute," said the other professor. With a knowing look, he went to the center and took an envelope from the top of the cabinet. This he **then** brought to Professor Wilson, saying, "Don't misplace these notes again."

Professor Wilson, happy at being relieved of her anxiety, seized the envelope and said gratefully, "Thank you so much. I promise never to **lose** them again—at least not today."

Lesson 27—Sweet Potato Casserole

Note: The six spelling corrections are printed in bold type.

Mrs. Britney's Sweet Potato Casserole

4 medium sweet **potatoes**
Vegetable oil spray
1/4 teaspoonful nutmeg
2 **tablespoonfuls** chopped walnuts
1/4 cupful of orange juice

Cook whole sweet **potatoes** in boiling water 25 to 30 minutes or until tender. Meanwhile, preheat oven to 375 degrees. Lightly spray a 1-quart casserole dish with vegetable oil spray.

Remove **potatoes** from heat, and add cold water until **potatoes** are cooled slightly. Peel and mash. Add remaining ingredients, and mix thoroughly. Place in casserole dish, and bake uncovered 25 minutes.

Serve hot. Garnish with **tomatoes**.

Part 5

Lesson 28—Word Games for Better Words

Answers. rise above, dog, begin, lie, goal, understand; oatmeal, puffed rice, chair, desk, bookcase, bed, school, house, garage, barn; 1. c 2. a 3. b

Lesson 29—A Matching Exercise

Answers. 1. a 2. c 3. e 4. ✓ 5. e 6. c 7. d 8. b 9. ✓ 10. a

Lesson 30—Our National Parks

Note: Corrections are underlined and in bold type. Students may have chosen to correct some sentences in different ways. An *E* indicates that the sentence is effective.

1. Olympic National Park has effective glacier-capped mountains, rainforests, **and old-growth** trees.
2. We **had to wait only** ten minutes to see Old Faithful erupt.
3. When visiting Gettysburg, **I thought of** President Lincoln's famous speech.
4. **While eating pancakes** at Carlsbad Caverns, we watched 300,000 bats dive into a cave.
5. At Lassen Volcanic National Park, every type of volcano on Earth can be seen. E
6. Her goals were to hike the Appalachian Trail and **to visit** Mount Rushmore.
7. As a student volunteer, you can dig for fossils in Badlands National Park. E
8. At Assateague Island, we **glimpsed not only** wild horses but also sika deer.
9. While snorkeling at Everglades National Park, **we saw** three manatees.
10. **Emma said, "Julie, I** might like to see Devil's Tower."

Lesson 31—Improve a Letter

Answers. 1. B 2. A 3. B 4. D 5. B and D 6. C 7. D

Lesson 32—Write Effective Paragraphs

Answers. 1. Students should have made notes for a sketch of their life or a family member's life. Students should have tried to think of at least five details for each paragraph. 2. Students should have chosen two of the topic sentences listed in the activity and should have expanded each into a paragraph. Students should have tried to include at least five details in each paragraph. 3. Students should have chosen one of the listed topics and should have written several paragraphs on it.

Lesson 33—Get the Facts

Answers. 1. Students should have found the information requested and should have listed the books of Internet sources they consulted. 2. Students should have researched one of the listed topics and should have found at least three authoritative sources that they could use to write a three- to five-page paper.

Lesson 34—Write an Essay

Answers. Students should have written a three- to five-page essay on the topic that they selected in Step 2 of the Lesson 33 Apply It! activity.

Lesson 35—Revise and Format an Essay

Answers. 1. Students should have revised the essay they wrote in the Lesson 34 Apply It! activity using the checklist presented at the beginning of the lesson and appropriate features of their word processing software. 2. Students should have formatted the revised essay using the formatting guidelines presented in the lesson and appropriate features of their word processing software. 3. Students should have proofread their essay using the steps and guidelines for proofreading given in the lesson and should have made any needed corrections.